GRIPPED BY THE GREATNESS OF GOD

JAMES MACDONALD

WITH LEARNING ACTIVITIES BY CLAUDE V. KING

LifeWay Press®
Nashville, Tennessee

ISBN 978-1-4158-2919-6
Item 001288990

Dewey decimal classification: 231.4
Subject headings: GOD—ATTRIBUTES\DISCIPLESHIP

To order additional copies of this resource, write to LifeWay Christian Resources
Customer Service; One LifeWay Plaza; Nashville, TN 37234-0133; fax (615) 251-5933;
phone toll free (800) 458-2772; e-mail *orderentry@lifeway.com*; order online at
www.lifeway.com; or visit the LifeWay Christian Store serving you.

Image credits: cover, Image 100 Ltd. and LifeWay photo; pp. 21 and 46, *Biblical Illustrator*
archive; p. 42, NASA and The Hubble Heritage Team; all others, Jupiter Images Corp.

Printed in the United States of America

Leadership and Adult Publishing
LifeWay Church Resources
One LifeWay Plaza
Nashville, TN 37234-0175

CONTENTS

ABOUT THE AUTHOR

James MacDonald is the pastor to 7,000 members of Harvest Bible Chapel in the northwestern suburbs of Chicago, Illinois. He was called as the first pastor of the church by 18 founding members in 1988. Now the church worships on three different campuses every weekend.

In addition to pastoring a rapidly growing congregation, James proclaims God's Word daily on the nationwide radio broadcast of *Walk in the Word*. His mission is to "ignite passion in the people of God through the proclamation of truth." As a result of a recent merger, James is now a Bible-teaching partner with Radio Bible Class Ministries in Grand Rapids, Michigan. James is also an author and a popular conference speaker.

James, a native of Canada, was ordained to the gospel ministry by Riverside Baptist Church in Windsor, Ontario. He is a graduate of London Baptist Bible College, Trinity Evangelical Divinity School, and Phoenix Seminary.

James's best friend and colaborer in ministry is his wife, Kathy. Married for 22 years, they have three children—Abby, Landon, and Luke.

OTHER BOOKS BY JAMES MACDONALD

Always True: God's Promises When Life Is Hard small-group study (LifeWay Press, 2011)
Always True: God's Five Promises for When Life Is Hard (Moody Publishers, 2011)
Ancient Wisdom (B&H Publishing Group, 2006)
Downpour: He Will Come to Us like the Rain small-group study (LifeWay Press, 2006)
Downpour: He Will Come to Us like the Rain (B&H Publishing Group, 2006)
God Wrote a Book (Crossway Books, 2002)
Gripped by the Greatness of God (Moody Publishers, 2005)
I Really Want to Change ... So, Help Me God (Moody Publishers, 2000)
Lord, Change My Attitude small-group study (LifeWay Press, 2008)
Lord, Change My Attitude ... Before It's Too Late (Moody Publishers, 2001)
Seven Words to Change Your Family (Moody Publishers, 2001)
When Life Is Hard small-group study (LifeWay Press, 2010)
When Life Is Hard (Moody Publishers, 2010)

Visit *www.lifeway.com/jamesmacdonald* for information about James MacDonald resources published by LifeWay.

INTRODUCTION TO GRIPPED BY THE GREATNESS OF GOD

Follow the session plans in the leader guide on page 139.

DVD Message Notes on Introduction to *Gripped by the Greatness of God* (28 minutes)

1. Who is Isaiah?
   - Isaiah ministered about _____ B.C. to affluent leaders of his day.
   - He ministered without compromise in a day of _____ decline.
   - From his pen come our most treasured prophecies concerning _____.

2. What does it mean to be gripped by God's _____?
   - To fall on our faces in solemn sweet surrender at the clear, unmistakable revelation of God and who He is
   - To be taken and shaken at the core of my being
   - To be captured in my heart with the reality of who God is so that I cannot, so that I will not ever be the same again!

3. How will this study affect my life?
   - Being gripped by God will transform your soul: your _____, your emotions, and your _____.

4. Is it possible? Hosea 6:3; James 4:8; Jeremiah 29:13

(Message Notes blanks: 740, moral, Christ, greatness, mind, will)

Responding to the Message

1. Why are we going to be looking at God's greatness in Isaiah?
2. How would you describe what it means to be gripped by God? In what way do you long to be gripped by Him?
3. Preview the topics for weeks 2-7 on page 3. Which one are you most looking forward to studying and why?

GRIPPED BY THE GREATNESS OF GOD

Welcome to our study of *Gripped by the Greatness of God*. I'm fired up about the opportunity to spend five days a week studying the Bible with you. I'm even more fired up about our topic. Each week I will open up God's Word to a mountaintop passage in the Book of Isaiah where we will see some of the most amazing things about our great God. My prayer is that you will be gripped by God's greatness.

At the beginning of each daily Bible study, I'll guide you to take a "Walk in the Word," meditate on a name of God from Scripture, and talk to the Lord in prayer. This will help you get your mind focused on God.

🖋 **Read Today's Walk in the Word verse in the margin, meditate on God's name, and talk to the Lord in prayer as you begin.**

Learning Activities and Prayer
Did you do what the activity directed you to do? This book may be different than other books with which you are familiar. Throughout the study, I'll be interacting with you through questions and learning activities. I also will be guiding you to interact with God through prayer. When I give you an assignment, take the time to do it so you will be able to gain the greatest impact on your life and thinking. That's what we're after—to be *gripped* by God.

Key Verse to Memorize
Each week I'll recommend a key verse of Scripture for you to memorize. When you are memorizing Scripture, read it several times. Meditate on it's meaning for you. Break it down into shorter segments. Write it on a card for review and review it daily. I'll get you started each week and remind you daily to review your memory verse.

① **Psalm 48:1 (Today's Walk in the Word) is a wonderful expression of praise for you to memorize this week. Begin memorizing it now by filling in the blanks below.**

"_____ is the _____, and _____ to be _____, in the _____ of our God, His _____ _____."

As you may have already guessed, this first week is going to be different than the rest of the weeks. It is shorter because we're getting oriented to our study of God's greatness. I'll be guiding you

Today's Walk in the Word
Psalm 48:1— *"Great is the Lord, and greatly to be praised, In the city of our God, His holy mountain."*

Meditate on God's Name
Lord God Almighty
(Revelation 4:8, KJV)

Talk to the Lord
Dear Lord God Almighty, You are great and greatly to be praised. I praise You and worship You today. As I begin this study of Your greatness, open my eyes to see and open my mind to understand Your greatness, Your majesty, Your splendor, and Your glory. Grip me with Your greatness. Amen.

to preview the messages for our study to whet your appetite for what's ahead. Next week we will dig in to a study of God's holiness.

② **Take a few minutes to browse through next week's lessons and get an idea of what is in store. Watch for each of the following features and check them off below as you find them.**

❑ Discussion Guide, DVD Message Notes, Responding to the Message (pp. 12-13). This two-page spread will guide your small-group session each week. Your leader also will use the leader guide to help you process what you are learning. Each week I will visit with your group by way of a DVD message. If you are not in a small group, I'd recommend you get with one or more people and study these messages together. There are some things about God we experience best when we are together with other believers (Matt. 18:19-20).

❑ Preview Statements, Snapshot Summary, My Goal for You, Key Verse to Memorize (p. 13). These items will give you a quick preview of the coming week's study.

❑ This Week's Mountaintop in Isaiah (p. 13). This is our Scripture focus for the week. You can use this text during the DVD message, if you like. In most cases you will need your Bible for the complete text to be used throughout the week.

❑ It Happened to Me (p. 14). I'm not teaching you theory only. Each week I'll tell you a brief story of how I have been gripped by the greatness of God.

❑ *Holiness* and *Transcendent* in the margin (p. 15). Occasionally I will define a word for you in the margin. I hope these help.

❑ In the margin you will also find Scriptures that have been referenced in the text and quotes that have been pulled out to the margin to emphasize key points (see p. 22). Take time to read the Scriptures. I've included them to save you time from looking them up in your own Bible. Let God's Word be planted in your mind. (Did you read Matthew 18:19-20 above?)

❑ At the end of each week you will find a closing prayer like the one on page 33. Make these personal as you read and pray them. The leaf icon (🍃) will alert you to an activity that guides you to interact with God in prayer. Don't skip the prayer activities. They may be the times where God grips you the most significantly.

③ **Turn to page 13 and read "This Week's Mountaintop in Isaiah—Isaiah 6:1-7." Watch for two gripping experiences in Isaiah's life. Write a *1* beside the time Isaiah is gripped with His sinfulness in light of God's holiness. Write a *2* beside the time he is gripped by God's forgiveness.**

🍃 **Close today's study in a prayer of petition to your Heavenly Father. Ask Him to begin gripping you with His greatness. Pray for the other members of your small group that they too would be gripped by God's greatness**

Matthew 18:19-20—" 'Again *I say to you, that if two of you agree on earth about anything that they may ask, it shall be done for them by My Father who is in heaven. For where two or three have gathered together in My name, I am there in their midst.' "*

DAY TWO *Being Gripped by God*

🍃 **Read Today's Walk in the Word verse in the margin, meditate on God's name, and talk to the Lord in prayer as you begin.**

Today's Walk in the Word
Isaiah 66:2— " 'My hand made
all these things,
Thus all these things came into
being,' declares the LORD.
'But to this one I will look,
To him who is humble and
contrite of spirit, and who
trembles at My word.' "

Meditate on God's Name
KING OF KINGS, AND LORD
OF LORDS (Revelation 19:16)

Talk to the Lord
My Lord and King, I worship
You today. You've made
everything I see. What a great
and creative God You are. I'm
amazed. Teach me during the
coming weeks to tremble at
Your Word and grip my heart
with a passion for You. Help me
be humble and contrite of spirit
also. Amen.

Review Your Memory Verse
Psalm 48:1—*"Great is the LORD,
and greatly to be praised.
In the city of our God, His
holy mountain."*

A couple of years ago I longed to see God grip the hearts of folks in our church. I loved them too much to see them live apart from the grasp of God upon them. To this end, I chose to teach what I believe are some of the most gripping passages in Scripture. And now, I'm grateful for the privilege of sharing these truths with you.

We are not seeking the dramatic or bizarre—we long for the unmistakable, the genuine unveiling of the glory of God. That kind of experience happens when God penetrates our hearts through the truth of His Word and the presence of His Spirit and drives the indifference and complacency from our souls. Being gripped by God's greatness will impact your life in three ways.

① **As you read the following paragraphs, circle the three ways.**

Being Gripped Involves Your Mind
When God reveals Himself in some way, the time is meant to give you a fresh awareness of His reality and nearness. Being gripped by God means you don't stay in spiritual kindergarten all your life. You grow in your knowledge of God and His Word.

Being Gripped Involves Your Emotions
When God gets a grip on your life, you feel something. In Scripture, every time someone has a genuine encounter with God, they are on their faces before Him. It's like a veil drops from their eyes, and they gasp at how great, and how close, and how real He is. Expect some tears, some joy, some awe, reverence, fear, and a host of other emotions as you experience God's greatness.

Being Gripped Involves Your Will
God is not simply about giving goose bumps. When He does get a grip on you, it's so you will do something differently. Does your will spring into action at every command of the Lord? As you study God's Word, are you asking, "Lord, what must I do"? The one God blesses is the one who does His will. Every week part of our study will focus on responding to God, doing something about what we've learned.

🍃 **Close today's lesson in prayer. Ask Him to grip your mind, your emotions, and your will. Think about the last time or the most significant time you were gripped by God and thank Him for revealing Himself to you.**

DAY THREE *Previewing Weeks 2 and 3*

🌿 **Read Today's Walk in the Word verses in the margin, meditate on God's name, and talk to the Lord in prayer as you begin.**

One Day at a Time

Is this your third day to study *Gripped by the Greatness of God*? Or are you already cramming to prepare for your next small-group session? Part of the value of a daily study is the time between lessons when God works and speaks during the course of the day. If you don't space the lessons out during the week, you may miss some of the deeper things of God that don't come in a rushed time. Do your best to study one lesson each day.

Today I want you to preview Weeks 2 and 3 about God's holiness and His awesomeness.

① **You've already browsed through Week 2. I want you to take a closer look today to preview it more carefully. Turn to pages 12-13. Read the following items and identify one thought or reason you will look forward to studying God's holiness.**
❏ DVD Message Notes on God's Holiness
❏ Preview Statements for This Week's Study
❏ Snapshot Summary, Goal, and Key Verse to Memorize
❏ This Week's Mountaintop in Isaiah—Isaiah 6:1-7

Reason I will look forward to studying God's holiness:

_____

② **Turn to pages 34-35 and preview Week 3. Read the following items and identify one thought or reason you will look forward to studying this topic.**
❏ DVD Message Notes on God's Awesomeness
❏ Preview Statements for This Week's Study
❏ Snapshot Summary, Goal, and Key Verse to Memorize
❏ This Week's Mountaintop in Isaiah—Isaiah 40

Reason I will look forward to studying God's awesomeness:

_____

🌿 **Close today's lesson in prayer. Ask God to reveal His holiness and awesomeness to you and ask Him to grip you as you participate in this study.**

Today's Walk in the Word
Isaiah 11:1-3— *"Then a shoot will spring from the stem of Jesse,*
And a branch from his roots will bear fruit.
And the Spirit of the LORD will rest on Him,
The spirit of wisdom and understanding,
The spirit of counsel and strength,
The spirit of knowledge and the fear of the LORD.
And He will delight in the fear of the LORD.

Meditate on God's Name
The Majesty on high (Hebrews 1:3)

Talk to the Lord
Lord, You are majestic—more than I can comprehend. But I ask You to fill me with Your Spirit—the spirit of wisdom, understanding, counsel, strength, knowledge, and the fear of the Lord so I can know You better. I delight to learn about You. Be my Teacher today. Amen.

Review Your Memory Verse
Psalm 48:1—*"Great is the LORD, and greatly to be praised.*
In the city of our God, His holy mountain."

DAY FOUR *Previewing Weeks 4 and 5*

🌿 **Read Today's Walk in the Word verses in the margin, meditate on God's name, and talk to the Lord in prayer as you begin.**

Today's Walk in the Word
Isaiah 12:4-6—*"And in that day you will say,*
'Give thanks to the LORD, call on His name.
Make known His deeds among the peoples;
Make them remember that His name is exalted.'
Praise the LORD in song, for He has done excellent things;
Let this be known throughout the earth.
Cry aloud and shout for joy, O inhabitant of Zion,
For great in your midst is the Holy One of Israel."

Meditate on God's Name
Him who is able to keep you from stumbling (Jude 24)

Talk to the Lord
Lord, I do praise You and give You thanks today. You have done excellent things. I continue to ask You to grip me with Your greatness and never let me go. Amen.

Review Your Memory Verse
Psalm 48:1—*"Great is the LORD, and greatly to be praised.*
In the city of our God, His holy mountain."

God's Word Is Your Lamp and Light
How are you doing at memorizing Psalm 48:1? Let me remind you of why Scripture memory is for your benefit. The psalmist said, "Thy word is a lamp to my feet, and a light to my path" (Ps. 119:105). God has provided His Word to guide and direct your life. Without it, you will wander aimlessly, miss His path, or go astray. The psalmist went on to say, "Thy word I have treasured [or hid] in my heart, that I may not sin against Thee" (Ps. 119:11). You will not always have your Bible available when temptation comes. Hiding His Word in your mind prepares you to resist temptation and avoid sin. Make Scripture memory a practice.

Today I want you to preview Weeks 4 and 5.

① **Turn to pages 54-55 and preview Week 4. Read the following items and identify one thought or reason you will look forward to studying God's sovereignty.**
❑ DVD Message Notes on God's Sovereignty
❑ Preview Statements for This Week's Study
❑ Snapshot Summary, Goal, and Key Verse to Memorize
❑ This Week's Mountaintop in Isaiah—Isaiah 45:1-13

Reason I will look forward to studying God's sovereignty:

_____

② **Turn to pages 76-77 and preview Week 5. Read the following items and identify one thought or reason you will look forward to studying God's works.**
❑ DVD Message Notes on the Works of God
❑ Preview Statements for This Week's Study
❑ Snapshot Summary, Goal, and Key Verse to Memorize
❑ This Week's Mountaintop in Isaiah—Isaiah 55

Reason I will look forward to studying the works of God:

_____

🌿 **Close this lesson in prayer. Ask God to reveal His sovereignty and His works to you and ask Him to grip you as you participate in this study.**

DAY FIVE *Previewing Weeks 6 and 7*

🌿 **Read Today's Walk in the Word verses in the margin, meditate on God's name, and talk to the Lord in prayer as you begin.**

Today I want you to preview Weeks 6 and 7 about worship and your identity in God. Next week we start digging in deep. Get ready!

① **Turn to pages 96-97 and preview Week 6. Read the following items and identify one thought or reason you will look forward to studying about worship that God ignites.**
   ❏ DVD Message Notes on the Worship of God
   ❏ Preview Statements for This Week's Study
   ❏ Snapshot Summary, Goal, and Key Verse to Memorize
   ❏ This Week's Mountaintop in Isaiah—Isaiah 58:1-11

Reason I will look forward to studying Gripped by the Worship of God:

_____

② **Turn to pages 116-117 and preview Week 7. Read the following items and identify one thought or reason you will look forward to studying about your identity in God.**
   ❏ DVD Message Notes on My Identity in God
   ❏ Preview Statements for This Week's Study
   ❏ Snapshot Summary, Goal, and Key Verse to Memorize
   ❏ This Week's Mountaintop in Isaiah—Isaiah 43:1-21

Reason I will look forward to studying my identity in God:

_____

🌿 **Close your study in prayer. Pray the following prayer slowly and make it your own.**

> Great God, Lord of the Universe and Lover of my soul—I come to this study feeling a bit nervous and curious at what I will discover about You. But I come. I come because I cannot stay away. I come in humility and anticipation of a fresh beginning with You. I'm not satisfied to follow man's dusty, diluted version of You. I want the real thing. All of You.
>
> So here is all of me. Grip my heart with Your greatness so I am never the same. I invite Your Spirit to meet me in these pages. In Your Holy name I pray. Amen.

Today's Walk in the Word
Isaiah 43:18-19—" 'Do not call
   to mind the former things,
Or ponder things of the past.
'Behold, I will do something new,
Now it will spring forth;
Will you not be aware of it?
I will even make a roadway
   in the wilderness,
Rivers in the desert.' "

Meditate on God's Name
Alpha and the Omega,
the beginning and the end
(Revelation 21:6)

Talk to the Lord
Lord, I'm ready and eager to be gripped in a fresh way by Your greatness. I'm not satisfied with my past experiences, I ask You to do something new. And not just for me, Lord ... grip the other members of my group. Grip my church. Don't leave us where we are. Flow into our lives like rivers in the desert! Amen.

Write Your Memory Verse
Psalm 48:1—

_____

_____

_____

_____

GRIPPED BY THE GREATNESS GOD OF

GRIPPED BY THE HOLINESS OF GOD

Follow the session plans in the leader guide on page 139.

Discussion Guide for the Introduction

1. In groups of 6-8 share your most memorable experience of being gripped by God's greatness:
   - a time when you experienced God's Word, His presence, or His work in a meaningful way;
   - OR a time when you emotionally or spiritually were overwhelmed with an understanding of who God is or what He does.
2. As a group, pause to pray sentence prayers of praise, worship and thanksgiving for the ways God has revealed Himself to you. Ask Him to grip you again during the upcoming study.

DVD Message Notes on God's Holiness (20 minutes)

1. We stink at finding _____ in the mirror. We have lost this view of God's holiness.
2. _____ means separateness, set apart, different.
3. Isaiah saw the pre-incarnate _____ (John 12:41, 1:18; Col. 1:15-20).
4. The _____ has lost its moral vision because it has lost its lofty and exalted view of God.
5. God's holiness demanded that sin be paid for, and then His _____ found a way.
6. True contact with God always produces an overwhelming sense of our own _____.

Responding to the Message

1. What are some of the things you learned about God's holiness?
2. Why do God's people need to understand and experience God's holiness today? What difference do you think it would make if we were to experience God in all His holiness?
3. If Isaiah were alive today and he were to declare, "I am a man of _____ and I dwell among a people of _____," what sins do you think he would name to God? What are some of the most common sins in society? Which ones would also be found among those who claim the name "Christian"?

Preview Statements for This Week's Study

- Holiness is character before it is ever conduct. It is the very nature of God reproduced in the heart of man.
- The process of holiness is the pathway to happiness.
- Every time God says "Don't," what He really means is "Don't hurt yourself."
- God displays holiness as the central and defining essence of His character.
- God's holiness demanded that sin be paid for and then His love compelled Him to pay the price Himself.
- A true glimpse of God in all His holiness will rock your world to the core.
- How many times have we said we want to know God? Here's our chance.
- In the purity of God's holiness, our sinfulness is exposed for public inspection.
- We are only prepared to receive and comprehend the grace of God when we have understood His infinite holiness and our incredible sinfulness.
- It's the holiness of God that casts us upon His mercy.
- Allow God to grip your heart with this truth and you'll find you have no more patience for your own lame excuses!

Snapshot Summary

God's holiness separates us from Him and yet compels us to be like Him.

My Goal for You

I want you to understand some of the dimensions of God's holiness and be so gripped by Him that you worship Him and seek to become like Him.

Key Verse to Memorize

Isaiah 6:3— *"'Holy, Holy, Holy, is the LORD of hosts, The whole earth is full of His glory.'"*

(Message Notes blanks: sin, Holiness, Christ, church, love, sinfulness)

This Week's Mountaintop in Isaiah—*Isaiah 6:1-7*

In the year of King Uzziah's death, I saw the Lord sitting on a throne, lofty and exalted, with the train of His robe filling the temple. Seraphim stood above Him, each having six wings; with two he covered his face, and with two he covered his feet, and with two he flew. And one called out to another and said, "Holy, Holy, Holy, is the LORD of hosts, The whole earth is full of His glory."

And the foundations of the thresholds trembled at the voice of him who called out, while the temple was filling with smoke. Then I said, "Woe is me, for I am ruined! Because I am a man of unclean lips, And I live among a people of unclean lips; For my eyes have seen the King, the LORD of hosts." Then one of the seraphim flew to me with a burning coal in his hand, which he had taken from the altar with tongs. And he touched my mouth with it and said, "Behold, this has touched your lips; and your iniquity is taken away, and your sin is forgiven."

It Happened to Me

A real turning point in my life came on a beach on the south coast of France. The year was 1998, and I was 38 years old. I had logged 10 years as a senior pastor. Our elder board, sensing my complete exhaustion, had graciously allowed us a 3-month sabbatical. I got as far away from the pressures of ministry as I could—a beach in France.

In that place of rest I could finally bring God the questions that were quenching my heart. *Why are people who claim to love You so harsh and unforgiving? Is it right that people so aggressively and ungratefully harvest the benefits of a person's strengths and then so vocally lament their weaknesses too? Man, why don't they get a mirror and take a look at their own lives?*

This hurt was coming from just a few people; by far the majority of people I was working and worshiping with were wonderful in every way. But those few made me sick of the "heat." And that summer I wanted "out of the kitchen." If I did go back, it would be to something very different.

I was weary and wondering how I could go on with such fear in my heart. Yes, I was scared, so much so that I hadn't even told my wife the depth of my disillusionment. But I had sure told the Lord. I came to Him with all my despair. I was looking for comfort but instead I found conviction ... about the sin of people pleasing. I was searching for hope, and God showed me His holiness. First slowly, and then with strength and supernatural force, God gripped my heart with His holiness.

Early one morning I was walking on the beach, listening to Scripture, and pouring out my heart to God. God's Spirit spoke to my spirit in a way that couldn't be any clearer if it was audible. His questions began to displace my own perplexities. *"Why are you so focused on others? Am I not the One you have chosen to serve?"* Jesus words to Peter in John 21 came with force, "What is that to you? Follow Me!" (v. 22). And the Lord said to me, *"Yes, others are hypocritical, but are you not the same? Do you practice all that you preach? Are you so far above others that you cannot give grace as I give it to you? I am the standard! Holiness is My nature and you're not coming close!"*

In a matter of moments I was on my face in the sand behind some rocks, spilling my tears into the ocean. I saw the Lord "high and lifted up." Not the God of the quick answer and the catchy praise chorus. Infinite, unapproachable holiness. As the waves crashed on the shore in the background of my hearing, wave after wave of God's holiness crashed upon my heart. What right do I have to question His calling? I have no choices—only to trust and obey a God who miraculously even takes notice of one like me.

God's holiness became my goal and consuming purpose—not managing human opinion, not keeping a record of wrongs, not juggling private sin and personal rationalizations. All these were lessons this preacher should know and did, but I needed to be gripped. I needed God's Spirit to take me and shake me about real holiness. The God-kind, pure and penetrating, powerful and infinite.

With the waves of realization came a deep heart commitment to give up "trying" to live the Christian life. That moment became a turning point for my whole understanding of how the holy character of God is formed in a believer.[1] I came to see that holiness is character before it is ever conduct. It is the very nature of God reproduced in the heart of man. It is the engine that fuels all lasting happiness. Christianity is not a prescription for behavior; it is a holy encounter.

Though I've since had my moments where human opinion has encroached, I was changed that day. I am stronger and more secure in my true purpose for existence. I was forever changed by the sea of holiness I saw on the south coast of France. Can a modern-day person be gripped by God's holiness? Yes, it happened to me.

DAY ONE *Get a Grip on God's Holiness*

🖋 **Read Today's Walk in the Word verse in the margin, meditate on God's name, and talk to the Lord in prayer as you begin today's study.**

① **I want to invite you to memorize Isaiah 6:3 (Today's Walk in the Word) as a wonderful statement of worship. Begin memorizing it and fill in the blanks below.**

" ' _____, Holy, _____, is the _____ of hosts,

the whole _____ is full of His _____.' "

Every journey begins with the first step. This first step in climbing the mountain of God's greatness means we walk in Isaiah's footsteps and see what Isaiah saw—the immense, indescribable, incomprehensible holiness of God. Maybe you're wondering why we can't start with something more friendly and then sort of work our way up to holiness. We don't get to choose where we start—God is in charge of that. So we'll start where God started with Isaiah—with His holiness.

② **Holiness. What thought does that word stir up in your mind? Check your response or write your own.**
- ❑ a. rules; a list of dos and don'ts
- ❑ b. the temple or tabernacle
- ❑ c. a refiner's fire, white hot
- ❑ d. a shouting preacher
- ❑ e. purity; white like snow
- ❑ f. other:_____

God's Holiness

Holiness means "separateness, sacredness, set-apartness." Isaiah's favorite name for God is "The Holy One of Israel." In using this name, Isaiah describes God's character in two seemingly opposite ways:

1. God is separate and transcendent, powerful, and intolerant of sin and rebellion. He is frightening beyond belief and filled with superhuman and potentially fatal power. God's holiness evokes awe and fear.
2. God is pure, righteous, perfect, and set apart from everything evil and unclean. He chooses to be near and engaged with His people to make them holy like He is holy. God's holiness evokes our adoration and reverence.

③ **Match the definition of God's holiness on the left with the emotions it evokes on the right.**

___ ___ 1. separate, powerful, intolerant of sin

___ ___ 2. pure, righteous, perfect

- a. adoration
- b. awe
- c. fear
- d. reverence

Today's Walk in the Word
Isaiah 6:3— " 'Holy, Holy, Holy, is the LORD of hosts, The whole earth is full of His glory.' "

Meditate on God's Name
The Holy One of Israel (Isaiah 1:4)

Talk to the Lord
Lord of hosts—the Holy One—You are holy … more holy than I can imagine. I confess that I'm somewhat fearful, but I also desire to be like You. Reveal Yourself to me this week and allow me to worship You. Open my spiritual eyes to see Your glory. Amen.

HOLINESS
separateness, sacredness, set-apartness

TRANSCENDENT
above and beyond, higher than the experience of our senses

As we study God's holiness this week, you may experience both sets of emotions. Fear and awe are appropriate emotions to have toward our holy God. Sin and impurity in your life should cause you to fear Him. But God's holy perfections are admirable. To adore Him, reverence Him, and desire to be like Him are also appropriate. Let's look at a New Testament passage that completes this truth. (The answers to the previous activity are 1-b,c; 2-a,d.)

> As obedient children ... like the Holy One who called you, be holy yourselves also in all your behavior; because it is written, "YOU SHALL BE HOLY, FOR I AM HOLY." ... knowing that you were not redeemed with perishable things like silver or gold from your futile way of life inherited from your forefathers, but with the precious blood as of a lamb unblemished and spotless, the blood of Christ (1 Pet. 1:14-19).

SAINTS
set apart ones; sanctified ones

John 17:15,17—" 'I do not ask You to take them out of the world, but to keep them from the evil one. Sanctify them in the truth; Your word is truth.' "

Called to Be Holy
As believers, we are called to be holy. We are called "saints"—literally "the set apart ones." The apostle Peter tells us to be like God—the Holy One—set apart in everything we do. He says, "Be totally sold out to God! Be available for His special use! Refuse to be entwined in sin." Jesus prayed for you in this same way (John 17:15,17). He asked His Father to protect you and to sanctify you (set you apart). Imagine that ... today, Jesus prays that you will be holy.

 Thank Jesus for praying for you. Ask Him to reveal this week anything in your life that is not in line with His holiness. Decide to obey His command to be holy. Ask Him to help you.

Contrary to popular opinion, God does not offer to forgive us simply so we can come to a crisis of conversion and receive the eternal benefits of His forgiveness. God cleanses us because He wants to transform us, to make us holy just as He is. So this infinitely holy, immeasurable, unalterable, unfathomable God says, "I've cleansed you for holiness." Think of that. "I want you to be like Me—holy. I've done what you could not do so you would have this incredible opportunity to be holy—now go for it."

Wow! "Be holy for I am holy." That's a high call. I cannot attain it. I feel like this silly little boy standing at the base of Mount Everest considering a climb. "Be holy for I am holy." You've got to be kidding; how could I ever ...?

 Close today's study by inviting God to grip you with His holiness this week. Invite Him to form His holiness in you. Choose to be holy as He is holy.

DAY TWO *The Essence of God's Character*

🌿 **Read Today's Walk in the Word verse in the margin, meditate on God's name, and talk to the Lord in prayer as you begin today's study.**

A Distorted View of Holiness

My earliest image of holiness is standing in a little country Baptist church. I was maybe five years old, staring straight ahead with my brothers, all stiff and stale, my suit and tie choking the life out of me. In the same row were my father, grandfather, and great-grandfather, each gripping the pew in front of them till their knuckles turned white. They sang at the top of their lungs "Holy, holy, holy, Lord God Almighty!"[2]

For me, God's holiness was connected with the clock ever so slowly ticking out the remaining minutes of the monotonous message while I squirmed on the hard seat searching for relief from the heat and longing to be free from constraint.

You may think of holiness as a list of rules to freeze freedom and crush your creativity. Maybe you have known people who claimed to be fired up about holiness, but there's nothing appealing about their lifestyle or perspective on living a God-centered life. They live by black-and-white thinking that says, "This is holy and that is not." Rule lovers delight to point out who is not making the grade on their latest checklist of absolute rules for holiness. That's not God's kind of holiness.

When I was a child, I didn't understand that the process of holiness is a pathway to happiness. I had to learn that God's holiness is not some abstract character trait to be admired like a fine painting or an antique car. What God forbids as sin He does because He knows us. Every time God says "Don't," what He really means is "Don't hurt yourself." When we choose to sin we choose to suffer. All the pain and suffering in our world is the result of humanity rejecting this call to holiness. But we can accept it today. We can embrace the reality of God's transforming work to genuine, lasting, joy-producing holiness. God knows this kind of joy infinitely and eternally.

① **Which of the following statements are distorted or inaccurate views of holiness. Check all that apply.**
   ❏ a. Holiness is legalistically living by a checklist of rules and commands.
   ❏ b. Holiness is a pathway to happiness.
   ❏ c. Holiness is God's way of limiting our freedom and stealing our fun.
   ❏ d. Holiness is what makes church services monotonous and boring.

Today's Walk in the Word
1 Peter 1:16—*"It is written, 'You shall be holy, for I am holy.'"*

Meditate on God's Name
God Most High, Possessor of heaven and earth (Genesis 14:19)

Talk to the Lord
O God Most High, the more I learn about Your holiness, the more I realize how high above me You are. To be holy like You is beyond my ability. Yet, you have commanded me to be holy like You. Surely, You must help me! I ask you to enable me to live a holy life like You have commanded. Amen.

Review Your Memory Verse
Isaiah 6:3— *"'Holy, Holy, Holy, is the Lord of hosts, The whole earth is full of His glory.'"*

> The process of holiness is a pathway to happiness.

God's True Character

Did you check a, c, and d? That's the way I read it. God does not present His holiness as a horizontal prescription for human activity. God displays holiness as the central and defining essence of His character. I know some people think God is defined by love, but I beg to differ. If love was at the very center of God's nature, then He could have welcomed us into heaven without the atoning death of His Son, Jesus. God's holiness demanded that sin be paid for, and then His love compelled Him to pay the price Himself.

> God's holiness demanded that sin be paid for, and then His love compelled Him to pay the price Himself.

② **Match the characteristic of God on the left with the corresponding action or description on the right. Write each letter beside a number.**

_____ 1. holiness

_____ 2. love

a. caused Jesus to pay the sin debt in our place on the cross

b. requires that sin be paid for

c. the defining essence of God's character

Holiness is the essence of God's character. (answers: 1-b,c; 2-a) To know God as He truly is requires dispelling our human notions of holiness and thinking about it in a fresh way. " 'Be holy for I am holy' " (Lev. 11:44). When we allow ourselves to be gripped by that reality, no human standard of goodness, no man-made regulation of righteousness, no plastic, legalistic creed will ever again substitute for such a fearful and wonderful encounter.

So let's bag what man says about God's holiness and let the ever-new message of God's Word shape our ideas about Him. The Bible has the power to change our lives by introducing us to a God who our culture, even our Christian culture, has ignored, softened, and minimized. A true glimpse of God in all His holiness will rock your world to the core.

③ **Do you want God to impact your world by revealing His holiness?**

❏ Yes   ❏ No, I'm not quite ready for that yet; but I'll keep reading.

Either way, will you stand with me at the base of God's holy mountain? Warning: There's no way we can scale the heights and fully understand holiness in this brief study or even in our short lifetime. After reading the next few pages, we won't say, "Oh, I get it. What's next?" But through the eyes and words of the prophet Isaiah, we can step a little closer. In humble dependence, we can ask God to reveal to us more of His holiness. I'm confident He will.

🖋 **Stop for a minute and pray. Ask God to reveal something of His holiness to you this week. Ask Him to open your mind to understand the Scriptures.**

Isaiah: Gripped by the Holiness of God

Isaiah flashed like a shooting star over the dark sky of a morally corrupt culture. His specific, God-given call was to minister to the affluent leaders of his day. Isaiah knew what it was like to move among self-sufficient people. They had power, money, and influence. What more did they need?

I talk to people all the time who have deceived themselves into thinking that they've got life hard-wired. They have good educations, good jobs, and good portfolios. Their lives are moving along at a pretty good pace, so they think they don't need God.

④ **Are you one of those people? Without saying it, do you think life is going so well that you really don't sense a need for God?**　❑ Yes　❑ No, I have a deep sense of needing God.

If I could, I would take these loved ones by the shoulders and shake them … hard. I would say, "Do you realize what you are saying?" But since it's not proper for a pastor to do that sort of thing, I'll settle for saying, "Wake up! It's not about who you are. It's all about who God is." That's what Isaiah figured out during the event recorded in Isaiah 6:1-7, our Scripture focus for this week.

God allowed Isaiah to peak into His heavenly throne room and glimpse His holiness like no human being has ever done! And Isaiah was seriously "gripped" by what he saw. Isaiah's vision of this scene is one we desperately need in the church today. Why? Because it blows away the comfortable, manageable God we've fashioned for ourselves. It reminds us how small we are and how great He is. So great in fact, that He is unapproachable except in the ways He has prescribed.

The Holy of Holies

Did you ever learn about the desert wanderings of the children of Israel? The people and priests understood God's innate holiness far better than we ever have. When God instructed them to build the tabernacle, He included a place for Himself called the holy of holies that was so sacred, so ominous only one person, once a year could enter and only with an offering. The place was filled with such mystery that every year, before that one priest entered, they would tie a rope of bells around his ankle, just in case he did something wrong and was struck dead on the spot. Then the other guys could pull him out of the holy of holies without meeting the same end. The priests of old had a mega, reverential awe of God and His holiness.

Back then nobody confused the creature and the Creator. God is holy, and to see His holiness meant to do things His way. God is set apart—way above any human standard. Set apart for a special purpose. There was no one like God. That's why this vision Isaiah had of entering God's throne room is so cool. And God invites us, through Isaiah's eyes, into a place very few people have ever been. How many times have we said we want to know God? Here's our chance! Tomorrow we'll start exploring Isaiah's vision one piece at a time.

How many times have we said we want to know God? Here's our chance!

Isaiah 6:3— "'Holy, Holy, Holy, is the LORD of hosts, The whole earth is full of His glory.'"

🖋 Close today's study with a time of prayer. Tell God what you've already learned about His holiness and worship Him for His greatness. Write out your memory verse as a prayer of worship to Him. Write it from memory or get some help in the margin.

_____

_____

_____

HOLINESS

DAY THREE *God on His Throne*

Today's Walk in the Word
Isaiah 5:16—*"The LORD of hosts will be exalted in judgment, And the holy God will show Himself holy in righteousness."*

Meditate on God's Name
Lord—Yahweh (Isaiah 1:2)

Talk to the Lord
Lord, You are holy and righteous, exalted. Guide me today to begin to grasp something of what that means. I know You are way beyond my understanding, but I do want to know You. Open my mind to understand Your holiness. Amen.

Review Your Memory Verse
Isaiah 6:3— "'Holy, Holy, Holy, is the LORD of hosts, The whole earth is full of His glory.'"

🖋 Read Today's Walk in the Word verse in the margin, meditate on God's name, and talk to the Lord in prayer as you begin today's study.

"In the year of King Uzziah's death" (v. 1)
The date 740 B.C. may not mean much to you and me, but to Isaiah's original readers, that year marked the end of an era. King Uzziah had been a fixture in Israel, ruling the nation for 52 years. For the most part, they had been good, peaceable, and prosperous years. But Uzziah's death came about as a result of an unusual experience. Uzziah died a painful death from leprosy.

① Read about Uzziah's experience in the temple that led to his developing the leprosy from which he later died. Circle the word that describes his attitude when he entered the temple.

> When he became strong, his heart was so proud that he acted corruptly, and he was unfaithful to the Lord his God, for he entered the temple of the Lord to burn incense on the altar of incense.
>
> Then Azariah the priest entered after him and with him eighty priests of the Lord, valiant men.
>
> And they opposed Uzziah the king and said to him, "It is not for you, Uzziah, to burn incense to the Lord, but for the priests, the sons of Aaron who are consecrated to burn

incense. Get out of the sanctuary, for you have been unfaithful, and will have no honor from the Lord God."

But Uzziah, with a censer in his hand for burning incense, was enraged; and while he was enraged with the priests, the leprosy broke out on his forehead before the priests in the house of the Lord, beside the altar of incense.

And Azariah the chief priest and all the priests looked at him, and behold, he was leprous on his forehead; and they hurried him out of there, and he himself also hastened to get out because the Lord had smitten him.

And Uzziah was a leper to the day of his death; and he lived in a separate house, being a leper, for he was cut off from the house of the Lord (2 Chron. 26:16-21).

Uzziah was proud. In arrogance he decided to burn incense for himself rather than depend upon the priests to do it for him. Against the counsel and opposition of 81 priests, he entered the sanctuary. And God smote him with leprosy. Talk about an experience of holiness! Early in his message, Isaiah said the proud will face a day of reckoning with the Lord (see Isa. 2:12,17). He knew that by firsthand observation.

② **Suppose you were Isaiah about to enter the temple for the first time after Uzziah's death from this leprosy. What do you think your attitude would be? Check your response or write your own.**
  ❏ a. Eager to worship. I love the Lord. I can't wait to enter His presence.
  ❏ b. Cool and calm. I'm not like Uzziah. I have nothing to fear.
  ❏ c. Cautious and reverent. This is a holy place, and God is a holy God.
  ❏ d. Fearful, terrified. Unholy people have died in this place. Am I really ready to enter God's presence?
  ❏ e. Other: _____

"I saw the Lord" (v. 1)

You may be calm or eager to enter into God's presence, but my guess is Isaiah was at least cautious and probably very fearful, if not terrified. Actually we're not told whether he was awake or sleeping, whether he had a vision in the temple or a dream about the temple. But Isaiah was supernaturally allowed to see the very throne room of God. Think of the significance of those four words. "I saw the Lord." Who could ever be the same?

Notice the word *Lord* in verse 1. When *Lord* is in all caps, it refers to God's covenant name, Yahweh. But here *Lord* is lowercase, referring not to God's name, but to His position as Ruler. Isaiah is really saying, "I saw the ultimate Monarch! I saw the Sovereign! The Ruler over everything! I saw Him!"

Isaiah 2:12—*"The LORD of hosts will have a day of reckoning Against everyone who is proud and lofty, And against everyone who is lifted up, That he may be abased."*

Isaiah 2:17—*"The pride of man will be humbled, And the loftiness of men will be abased."*

Model of the temple entrance

③ **Match the word on the left with the correct name or description on the right. Write each letter beside a number.**

___ ___ 1. Lord (cap and lowercase)   a. God's covenant name

                                         b. God's position as ruler

___ ___ 2. Lᴏʀᴅ (all caps)   c. Monarch, Sovereign

                                         d. Yahweh

John 12:41—*"Isaiah said this because he saw Jesus' glory and spoke about him" (NIV).*

Look back at the previous section to check your answers.

John 12:41 indicates that Isaiah actually saw the pre-incarnate Christ, the second Person of the Trinity. It couldn't have been God the Father, as is commonly thought, since John 1:18 says, "No one has seen God at any time; the only begotten God who is in the bosom of the Father, He has explained Him." Before Jerusalem, before Nazareth, before Bethlehem, Isaiah was given one glimpse of Jesus, the second Person of the Trinity in all of His glory … and it took his breath away.

"Sitting on a throne" (v. 1)

"I saw the Lord sitting on a throne." Sitting—not pacing back and forth. Sitting —not wringing His hands. Sitting—not struggling or searching. He was seated. He was settled. He was secure. He was certain.

I wrote in the margin of my Bible, "Why so settled and so seated?" Because He is in control. He knows it. Everyone in the throne room knows it. No one is worried.

I am struck by that truth each time we sing a particular worship song at Harvest Bible Chapel. The lyrics include the phrase, "You are in control." When I sing it, I think of this verse in Isaiah. God is seated on the throne. He is in control. That puts into perspective any burden I carry on my heart. How difficult could this problem be for God, no matter how monstrous it might seem to me? My problems are nothing to Him. He is in control!

> My problems are nothing to Him. He is in control!

④ **Think about the biggest problem you are facing right now. Write a word or phrase to identify it.**

_____

Is the Lord even in control of this? Yes! He's even controlling that.

⑤ **Think about the biggest problem facing the world right now. Write a word or phrase to identify it.**

_____

Even that? Yes! The Lord is sitting on His throne. He's in control.

"Lofty and exalted" (v. 1)

Notice the Lord isn't in some common or ordinary setting. "I saw Him sitting on a throne, lofty and exalted." I believe the main reason the church has lost its moral vision is because it has lost its high and exalted view of God. We have embraced the comfort of His nearness at the expense of His transcendence. God is not the "man upstairs." God is not an old codger with a white beard. God is ineffable glory and He dwells in unapproachable light. The Bible says that no one can see God and live. He is lofty and exalted.

"With the train of His robe filling the temple" (v. 1)

The train is the part of the robe that communicates honor. Seldom seen today except at formal weddings, the train is the symbol of grandeur and royalty. At the coronation of Queen Elizabeth many years ago at Westminster Abbey, the train of her robe went all the way down the aisle and almost to the back door of the cathedral.

What does Isaiah say about the robe of Almighty God? He says it fills the temple! Down the aisle and back again, back to front, front to back, doubling and redoubling. The symbol of God's splendor and honor fills the temple. So awesome is this view of God that Isaiah can look no higher than the train of His robe. Isaiah cannot elevate his eyes beyond the hem of our Lord's garment.

⑥ **Pause to praise God for His greatness. Confess the truths you are learning about His exalted status. Write the truths below as your prayer. I've included one for you.**

Lord, You are in control. I exalt You.

_____

_____

_____

"Seraphim stood above Him" (v. 2)

Isaiah is so completely awestruck that he has to look away, and says in affect with his next phrase, "Let me tell you about the angels." The seraphim are the angels that exist in the throne room who instantaneously do the bidding of Almighty God—ever standing to serve the seated Sovereign. The Hebrew word *seraph* literally means "the burning ones." Though we have more questions than we can answer about the seraphim, we are given a limited physical description of them and their role. "Each having six wings; with two he covered his face, and with two he covered his feet, and with two he flew" (v. 2).

Why six wings? Two cover their faces lest they see the glory of God and die—always serving but never able to look upon the Holy One. Two wings cover their feet which symbolize their lowliness—lest God see them and the shame they feel in the presence of infinite holiness. With two more wings they flew. It's interesting that four of their six wings are for relating to God; only two are for serving Him.

The verbs *covered* and *flew* indicate continuous action. The angels' motion is ceaseless as they fulfill with precision every wish of almighty God. And they don't just fly; they speak as they hover around God's throne.

TRANSCENDENCE
the state of being above and beyond, higher than the experiences of our senses

INEFFABLE
divine, beyond words, indescribable, heavenly

SERAPHIM
the burning ones, angels with six wings

⑦ **The message of the seraphim is found in your memory verse. Fill in the blanks below as a review of their message.**

" '_____, Holy, _____, is the _____ of hosts,

the whole _____ is full of His _____.' " –Isaiah 6:3

"And one called out to another ... 'Holy, Holy, Holy' " (v. 3)

Do you have that picture in your mind's eye of the seraphs forming two lines coming out from God's throne? Listen as they call out back and forth, from one line to the other in an antiphonal chorus that through eons of time has gone on without interruption. And what do they say? Imagine all the things they could say about God. They could say, "Merciful, merciful, merciful God!" They could say, "Loving, loving, loving God!" But God, in a mystery we could guess at but never comprehend, chose that the words spoken continuously before His throne would be of His holiness. So these burning ones call back and forth, back and forth, back and forth, never ceasing: " 'Holy, holy, holy is the LORD of hosts. The whole earth is full of His glory.' "

> There is great power in repetition, especially if the subject is an attribute of God.

When the truth is significant, there is great power in repetition, especially if the subject is an attribute of God. When someone writing or speaking in the Hebrew language wants to emphasize something, he or she will repeat the word. For example, *shalom*, the Hebrew word for peace used in Isaiah 26:3, is literally "peace, peace," meaning peace now and peace for eternity. This triple repetition is used only of God and only of this attribute. The seraphs are saying that God is not just holy, and not just "holy, holy," but that the Lord of hosts is "holy, holy, holy"! The whole earth is full of His glory! Isaiah stood there stunned and silent as he gazed upon the transforming scene and trembled in the presence of holy God.

"The foundations of the thresholds trembled" (v. 4)

Isaiah, no doubt prostrate by now, was not aware that the whole temple was shaking. It seems he thought just the doorway was shaking as if to say, "This far! No further! You can go no closer to the holy presence of Almighty God."

"The temple was filling with smoke" (v. 4)

Consider the scene. The angel's antiphonal hymn was thunderous. The temple foundation was shaking. Then came the smoke rising quickly to veil Isaiah's sight. Why smoke? I believe it was God's protection of Isaiah lest he be consumed in another moment by the utter terror, by the majestic purity and power, the unsearchable, unspeakable, infinite holiness of the Triune God. The smoke graciously shielded Isaiah from a view that no man or woman could see and live (Ex. 33:20).

Exodus 33:20—"'You cannot see My face, for no man can see Me and live!'"

Now, friend, when was the last time you heard about the incredible reality of God's holy presence? Have you ever fully considered what it means? Preferring the comforting truths of God's love and mercy, we have lost this awesome vision of His holiness. The result is that our faith is too often anemic and malnourished by the spiritual equivalent of junk food. We talk about Him as if He were our buddy. We wallow in sin and revel in a grace that is cheapened because it is separated from this penetrating, purifying holiness.

⑧ **Before you began this study, which of the following statements would have most nearly described your attitude toward God? Check one.**
   ❑ a. God is kind, loving, and merciful. He cuts me some slack when I'm not living according to His commands. He's cool.
   ❑ b. God is so far removed from me, I don't think He pays any attention to what I do. I have nothing to fear.
   ❑ c. God is holy and expects holy living from His children. I take my relationship with Him very seriously. I seek to obey Him. I want to be pure.

We've missed such a huge piece of what it means to be alive and to be men and women connected to God. When we experience God for who He really is, we suddenly see ourselves for who we are. We have no identity problem when we understand ourselves from God's perspective. Our anxieties and pressures dissipate. When we see God as Isaiah did here, we dip our toes in the greatest experience a human being can have—to stand in the presence of a holy God.

   We desperately need to be gripped by this view of the highness and the holiness of God. Because we have failed to let it capture our hearts, we seldom hear or see people confessing their sinful condition as Isaiah did in verse 5. We also seldom see people readily volunteering for service to the King as Isaiah did in verse 8.

⑨ **Using some of the words in the margin and others of your choosing, write a prayer, hymn, or poem of praise to God.**

_____

_____

_____

_____

_____

_____

_____

- almighty
- awesome
- beautiful
- enthroned
- exalted
- glory, glorious
- great
- hallowed
- high
- holy, holiness
- honored
- incredible
- indescribable
- ineffable
- infinite
- majestic, majesty
- noble
- powerful
- pure
- regal
- royal
- sacred
- separate
- set apart
- sovereign
- splendor
- transcendent
- triune
- unapproachable
- unsearchable
- unspeakable

DAY FOUR *Isaiah's Response to God's Holiness*

Today's Walk in the Word
Hebrews 12:14 (HCSB)—
"Pursue peace with everyone, and holiness—without it no one will see the Lord."

Meditate on God's Name
The LORD who sanctifies you (Exodus 31:13)
The LORD, who makes you holy (Exodus 31:13, NIV)

Talk to the Lord
What good news this is, Lord! You are the One who makes me holy. You set me apart for Yourself. I can't do this without Your help. But with Your help, I choose today to live a separated life. Help me stay away from things and thoughts that are unclean and impure. Develop in me a healthy and reverent fear of Your holiness and perfect that holiness in me. Amen.

Review Your Memory Verse
Isaiah 6:3— *" 'Holy, Holy, Holy, is the LORD of hosts, The whole earth is full of His glory.' "*

🌿 **Read Today's Walk in the Word verse in the margin, meditate on God's name, and talk to the Lord in prayer as you begin today's study.**

" 'Woe is me, for I am ruined!' " (v. 5)

Isaiah, watching all of this, finally had to say something. His only appropriate response to the impact of being gripped by God's holiness was " 'Woe is me, for I am ruined!' " (v. 5). The word *woe* means literally the calamity has fallen or is about to fall. Malachi 3:2 says, "Who can endure the day of his coming? And who can stand when He appears?" Isaiah was saying in effect, "That's God? That's who He is? I am dust!"

The same is true today. You cannot gaze upon the holiness of God without being overcome. Even as I recently studied this passage and reflected on God's holiness, I felt devastated by my own sinfulness. How could a person not be overcome when confronted with such a holy God? Isaiah was saying in effect, "That's the standard? That's how high the bar is set? If that's true, then I am finished! I am broken! Woe is me!"

I have to shake my head in grief when I hear people spout, "I don't know what God's doing in this ol' world, but if I ever get a chance, I'm gonna straighten Him out on a few things." And I want to respond, "What?! What did you say? Listen up! No one can see God and live!"

David said, "If You, LORD, should mark iniquities, O Lord, who could stand?" (Ps. 130:3). If God were to mark and record every sin we have committed, who could bear up under the scrutiny? So Isaiah says, " 'Woe is me, for I am ruined!' " Isaiah shouted in effect, "I'm dead. I'm done for. I am silenced."

① **Suppose you've just entered the temple where, not long ago, God struck arrogant King Uzziah with leprosy (and he died a slow and painful death). You see the Holy One, God Most High, and He sees you. You know His gaze penetrates past all your cover-ups. Nothing in your mind or in your past activities is hidden to Him. What would you say? Check one or write your own.**
❑ a. Great! I can't wait to tell Him about my latest achievements.
❑ b. Now's my chance to straighten Him out on a few things.
❑ c. Woe is me, I'm ruined. I'm done for!
❑ d. Other: _____

" 'I am a man of unclean lips' " (v. 5)

Are you gripped yet? Maybe you can identify a bit with our friend Isaiah. If ever for a moment we should get to peak under the corner of the curtain and into the holy of holies, we would be on our faces before God. Isaiah says, " 'Woe is me ... because I am a man of unclean lips.' "

"How can I open my mouth and speak for this God? What can I say about Him?" Isaiah asks. "I am a man of unclean lips. And I dwell among a people of unclean lips." We're all so truly sinful before this Holy God!

② **What is the first thing God would have already seen and known about you? What would your confession be? Fill in the blanks.**

Woe is me! I am a person of _____

and I dwell among a people of _____

Nothing is hidden from His sight. God forgive us for thinking, "You know, Lord, I think I'm a bit more holy than some of Your other followers." What a joke! Who cares about how you compare to the other guy? Who can stand before this God? May God forgive us for seeing this chapter title and thinking, "Holiness, oh yeah, maybe there's a couple of things I could dig out and upgrade, but I don't know what they are. I know I'm not perfect, but I've known the Lord for a long time and I've come pretty far in." In what? Who could gaze upon this God and not be overcome with a sense of their incredible, desperate need for a fresh infusion of who He is?

May God help us be a people who will embrace not only the messages about Him that delight our hearts, but also the ones that grip us and shake us to the core of our souls. We'll have to deal with these truths about God for all eternity, better to start the reality check now, don't you think?

🖋 **We don't have to be in such a rush that we don't have time with the God who is holy but who also loves us and wants to help us be holy as He is holy. Before we go further, stop to talk to the Lord about what you are feeling and thinking.**

" 'My eyes have seen the King' " (v. 5)

Isaiah said, "I'm ruined. I'm filthy. I live with unclean people." Why, Isaiah? Why do you feel so overcome? Because, the prophet writes, " 'My eyes have seen the King!' " The king of what? "The King!" It's like he said, "My eyes—for a moment before the temple filled with smoke—my eyes saw the King!" Isaiah grieved, "I saw the King, and I knew I was unclean."

What he discovered at a deeper level we all must continually review. We are all immensely unclean before the holiness and righteousness of

> Who could gaze upon this God and not be overcome with a sense of their incredible, desperate need for a fresh infusion of who He is?

Almighty God. In the purity of God's holiness, our sinfulness is exposed for public inspection.

"Then one of the seraphim flew to me" (v. 6)

One of the seraphim flew to Isaiah "with a burning coal in his hand, which he had taken from the altar with tongs. And he touched [Isaiah's] mouth with it and said, 'Behold, this has touched your lips; and your iniquity is taken away, and your sin forgiven'" (vv. 6-7).

There's an incredible lesson here. We are only prepared to receive and comprehend the grace of God when we have understood His infinite holiness and our incredible sinfulness. Any presentation of the gospel which leaves that truth out is incomplete. It's the holiness of God that casts us upon His mercy.

Notice that Isaiah didn't get the same response as King Uzziah. What made the difference? "'GOD IS OPPOSED TO THE PROUD, BUT GIVES GRACE TO THE HUMBLE'" (Jas. 4:6). Uzziah: proud. Isaiah: humble. Later in Isaiah's message we read more about this acceptable spirit:

> Thus says the High and Lofty One
> Who inhabits eternity, whose name is Holy:
> "I dwell in the high and holy place,
> With him who has a contrite and humble spirit,
> To revive the spirit of the humble,
> And to revive the heart of the contrite ones"
> (Isa. 57:15, NKJV).

③ **If God made a decision about how to respond to you based on this distinction, in what condition would He find you? Check one.**
❑ a. Arrogant, proud
❑ b. Humble, lowly, contrite

Are you disappointed with your response? Try to remember that the next time you are tempted to gloss over a sin in your life. "Well, it's not that bad." Or "everyone understands." Refuse trashy rationalizations. They belong in the gutter. Let's never forget Isaiah's throne room vision of the holiness of God. Allow God to grip your heart with this truth and you'll find you have no more patience for your own lame excuses!

God calls us to holiness. That's why that seraphim went to the altar and got a coal to cleanse Isaiah. God wants us to be holy. How incredible is that? "Be holy for I am holy," God says. "What? Like You? How could that be possible?" Isaiah, overcome with his own sinfulness, begins to experience the grace and mercy that flows from this holy throne. Forgiven!

The altar was a place of continual burning, where animals were offered as sacrifice for sin. Because of His holiness, God will not simply declare us righteous in some random act. He will not dismiss our sin without a substitute. It was on that altar where the substitute

---

It's the holiness of God that casts us upon His mercy.

CONTRITE
repentant, crushed, penitent, remorseful, sorrowful

for sin was made. For us that substitution was made on a cross at Calvary. That's a picture of our loving, forgiving, merciful God.

"He touched my mouth with it" (v. 7)

The angel comes with the coal and psssssssst. Purged. Maybe as you read this material you feel that you cannot possibly relate to this holy God. Perhaps there are some things you have done in your life that few, if any, people know about. You feel so ashamed, unclean, and unworthy. But aren't you amazed to discover that in the fullest and most awe-producing vision in all of Scripture regarding God's holiness there is this picture of His forgiveness?

God Himself sent for the instrument of Isaiah's cleansing and forgiveness. Isaiah was washed clean. Cleansed, not only of the small and silly but also of the serious and shameful. Wholly cleansed by our holy God.

④ **Reflect on your life. Are there actions or experiences for which you do not yet sense God's forgiveness and cleansing? If so, name those things to Him in prayer as He sits on His throne in heaven. Then read in the margin the wonderful promise found in Isaiah 1:18.**

Isaiah 1:18—"'Come now, and let us reason together,' Says the LORD, 'Though your sins are as scarlet, They will be as white as snow; Though they are red like crimson, They will be like wool.'"

Forgiveness in Jesus Christ

Up to this point, I've made an assumption that you have entered a saving relationship with Jesus Christ. But I realize that may not be true for you. I don't want to miss this opportunity to point you to that ultimate cleansing relationship that Jesus can provide for you.

I remember the first time I truly understood that God's holiness was entirely unattainable. That no matter how hard I tried I could never live up to this infinite standard. I learned that because of my sins I was not only ineligible for God's forgiveness, but I fully deserved His punishment. I was told that two thousand years ago Jesus Christ, God's Son, accepted the punishment for my sin and died in my place on the cross. I saw that Jesus gave His life so His holy Father could release me from the just penalty for my sin and grant to me full and complete forgiveness. To be truly forgiven, all I had to do was turn from my sin and come to Christ by faith. And I did just that.

⑤ **Have you come to that understanding? Have you turned from your sin and come to Christ by faith in what He did for you at the cross? Check your response.**
❏ Yes, I have repented of (turned from) my sin and placed my faith in Christ; and He has forgiven me.
❏ No, that is something I've never done.

⑥ **If your answer is yes, briefly describe in the margin the time you made that decision to turn from sin to Christ.**

If you have never made that decision, I urge you to do so now. All God longs to do in your life begins in that moment of conversion

Matthew 18:3—" 'Truly I say to you, unless you are converted [lit. are turned] and become like children, you will not enter the kingdom of heaven.' "

Romans 6:23—"The wages of sin is death, but the free gift of God is eternal life in Christ Jesus our Lord.

Romans 10:9—"If you confess with your mouth Jesus as Lord, and believe in your heart that God raised Him from the dead, you will be saved."

(Matthew 18:3). It's a crisis every person must come to, and it doesn't happen by accident. To be converted requires turning from sin and coming to God in faith that Jesus died for you.

What Isaiah experienced from the altar in that moment was symbolic of the sacrifice of Jesus once for all. And it can be yours in this moment if you embrace by faith the forgiveness God freely offers in Christ (Romans 6:23; 10:9).

🌿 **Close today's lesson in prayer. If you need and desire to turn to Jesus Christ in faith, you can do that now. Follow the steps listed below.**
- Confess to Jesus that you are sinful, that you need His forgiveness.
- Agree to turn away from your sinful ways and to Him and His ways.
- Ask Him to forgive you and trust Him to do it.
- If you need help, talk to a pastor or Christian friend.

🌿 **If you have already taken these steps, pray for those who may need to come to Christ by faith. Then, thank God for His mercy and forgiveness.**

DAY FIVE *Responding to God's Holiness*

Today's Walk in the Word
2 Corinthians 6:17–7:1—
" 'Come out from their midst and
   be separate,' says the Lord.
" 'And do not touch what
   is unclean;
And I will welcome you.
And I will be a father to you,
And you shall be sons and
   daughters to Me,'
Says the Lord Almighty.
Having these promises, beloved,
let us cleanse ourselves from
all defilement of flesh and spirit,
perfecting holiness in the fear
of God."*

🌿 **Read today's Walk in the Word verses in the margin on this page and onto the next, meditate on God's name, and talk to the Lord in prayer as you begin today's study.**

Are you gripped by the awesome reality of these truths about God? Will you let the holiness of our awesome God take you and shake you so that you never see temptation as tempting again? Begin by rejecting the kind of surface adjustments that substitute for holiness in so many corners of Christ's kingdom. This may be God's wake-up call to you. Or perhaps you need to examine if a hyper-grace mentality has eclipsed your vision of an exalted and holy God who is calling you to live a lifestyle that is truly set apart for Him. As you are forgiven and cleansed, I challenge you to be finished with rationalizations and hypocrisy. They have no place before a holy God! As we invite God to grip our lives with His holiness, let's respond to Him with a passionate pursuit of genuine Christlikeness. Together let's pursue lives and lifestyles that proclaim with integrity the infinite holiness of our great God.

① **Examine your daily habits with a willingness to change anything that doesn't reflect God's holiness. As things come to mind that need to change, make a list and begin to make the necessary adjustments. Holiness requires radical change.**
  - What do you need to lock out of your life? Perhaps some viewing habits on the Web, television, or video?
  - What do you need to change? Is it the way you spend your money or the way you respond to those who hurt you?
  - What do you need to limit—what is stealing your hunger for God?
  - What habits do you need to eliminate completely?

🍃 **What's been your take on holiness? Do you tend to be a rule-lover or does your pendulum swing more toward freedom and not enough behavioral boundaries? Consider what it means to be holy (set apart) for God in practical ways. Ask God to help you choose your convictions, attitudes, and actions based on His defining holiness.**

② **Consecrate your home. Pretend that Jesus Himself is preparing to visit. He's going to take a tour and carefully examine everything in every room. What is in your home that you would be ashamed for Jesus to see? Pray and ask the Holy Spirit to give you a sensitivity to Him, His holiness, His purity. Then take a walk through each room of your home with a trash bag and throw away everything that is unholy, impure, unclean, or unbecoming a follower of Jesus Christ. Use the points in activity 1 to help guide your time.**

Meditate on God's Name
Holy Spirit of God
(Ephesians 4:30)

Talk to the Lord
Holy Spirit of God, how grateful I am that You live in me. I want to increasingly die to sin and live a clean and pure life. Help me fix my mind on the things that are pure and holy. Strengthen me to resist temptation and honor You. Amen.

Write Your Memory Verse
Isaiah 6:3—

_____

_____

_____

_____

CASE STUDIES

Brandon is a traveling salesman. His work takes him on the road for days at a time, so he is frequently staying in hotels in his four-state territory. When he gets checked in after a busy day, he flips on the television and starts surfing channels. The hotels provide movies and channels that he doesn't permit in his home because of the graphic violence, sexual immorality, and nudity. In the privacy of his room, he lingers places he doesn't belong. Brandon realizes he is vulnerable when he is tired and alone. He's filled with a sense of guilt and shame at the impurity he's putting into his mind.

③ **If you were Brandon, what would you do to pursue holiness? Check your response or write your own.**
  - ❏ a. Get an accountability partner or group that will encourage me, pray for me, and challenge me to keep my mind pure.
  - ❏ b. Give up watching television and develop other activities that will be better for my spiritual health.
  - ❏ c. Spend more time on the phone with my wife and children and severely limit my television viewing.
  - ❏ d. Change jobs so I don't have to be on the road so much.
  - ❏ e. Other:_____

Joan is Brandon's wife. She's taken up reading romance novels to pass the time when he's out of town. Reading about the passionate encounters of others has begun stimulating her own fantasies. She catches herself daydreaming about relationships with other men. She realizes her thought life is getting out of control. Even though she's horrified at the thought, she's even dreamed about having an affair. She's become "addicted" to these novels and can't seem to put them down. The Holy Spirit has convicted her that things must change.

④ Joan has come to you for counsel. Assuming Brandon's schedule is not going to change, what would you suggest Joan do to clean up her thought life and prevent this from developing again? Make notes in the margin.

Oscar is a brand new Christian. His language is still much like the rest of the world's. He slips up and uses profanity occasionally. His joking around with coworkers is still crude. His eyes, mind, and heart are still filled with lust. He still catches himself lying at home and at work. His habit of drinking alcohol in excess is still a problem. But the Holy Spirit is bringing conviction about the lack of holiness in his life. He knows his life in Christ should be different from those who don't know Christ. He longs to change and experience victory in these areas of his life.

⑤ Oscar overhears that you are learning about the holiness of God and his interest is peaked. Here's his question to you: What have you learned about God and His holiness that can help me put away unholiness and live a holy life? Review this week's lesson. What key ideas would you teach him to help him begin making the changes he needs. Write notes in the margin or on a separate sheet of paper. Be prepared to share your ideas with your small group.

⑥ What are some other situations where Christians you know are challenged by unholy living? Check any you know to be true. List others you would describe as unholy.
   ❑ addiction to pornography
   ❑ involvement in sexually explicit chat rooms on the Internet
   ❑ drug or alcohol addiction
   ❑ crude joking, obscenity
   ❑ adultery
   ❑ gambling, greed
   ❑ unethical conduct in the workplace
   ❑ constantly pursuing pleasure and having little time for God
   ❑ treating the Lord's Day or the Lord's things in an unholy manner
   ❑ showing contempt for or disregard of God's Word or the body of Christ
   ❑ dishonesty, lying, stealing
   ❑ profaning God's name
   ❑ distorting marriage or family life in the eyes of a watching world
   ❑ Others: _____

⑦ Select one of the items you checked above and describe in the margin how you would counsel a brother or sister in Christ who is needing help to put off the unholy and be holy as God is holy.

⑧ This Sunday as you attend a worship service, imagine the scene Isaiah described of the Lord seated on His throne and in full control. Whatever burden you carried into the service, lay at His feet and direct your focus toward His majestic holiness. What burdens can you lay at His feet even now? He is in control.

_____

_____

_____

_____

Close this week's study with the following prayer, but take it slowly and personalize it. Say what you want to say to the Lord. If you are not ready to make these promises or commitments, invite God to help you develop a willingness to respond to Him.

> Holy God, please forgive me for my casual attitude about sin. Action sin. Thought sin. Speech sin. Forgive me, God, for hiding my behavior behind Your abundant grace. Help me to embrace from my heart a season of transformation. No more duplicity and hypocrisy. No more playing church and playing Christian. I want the real thing, Lord.
>
> Oh God, I want to see You reigning, not just upon Your throne but in my heart, in my life, in my home, and in my relationships. Pursue me with a desire for me to be like You that I cannot outrun. Be specific with me, God. I invite You to be high and lifted up reigning upon the throne of my heart. This I pray in Your name. Amen.

[1] James MacDonald, _I Really Want to Change … So, Help Me God: God's Power to Transform Lives_ (Chicago: Moody Publishers, 2000), 32.
[2] Reginald Heber, "Holy, Holy, Holy," _The Baptist Hymnal_ (Nashville: Convention Press, 1991), 2.

GRIPPED BY THE GREATNESS GOD OF

GRIPPED BY THE AWESOMENESS OF GOD

Follow the session plans in the leader guide on page 140.

Discussion Guide on God's Holiness

1. What have you learned OR experienced about holiness this week that has been most meaningful or life changing?
2. Turn to page 31, review each of the three case studies and discuss your responses to each one.
3. Turn to page 25 and invite several volunteers to read their prayer, hymn, or poem of praise to God (activity 9).
4. In same-sex groups of 2, 3, or 4 share what God is doing in your lives regarding holiness. Share a recent testimony of victory over sin, a major choice made while consecrating your home (p. 31), your struggle with pride, or an area of unholiness over which you need to win victory. Take time to pray for each person in your group that they will become holy as God is holy.

DVD Message Notes on God's Awesomeness (21 minutes)

1. Only God is _____.
2. God's two arms: God's arm of _____, power, and rule and God's tender and caring arm.
3. God sits above the _____ of the earth (v. 22).
4. We don't influence God's plans a bit.
5. Lest we are too hard on those who fashion physical _____, we have our own idols. We have things we substitute for God, things we put in the place of God. Nothing can substitute for God.

6. God's _____ are inexhaustible because He's awesome.
7. Are you tired, discouraged? Your problems aren't too big, your God is too _____.
8. Isaiah 40:31—Some things you can fly above. Some things you have to go through. Some things last for a lifetime.

Responding to the Message

1. Which description of God or His activity most impressed you with His awesomeness and why?
2. What are some of the modern-day idols Christians may substitute for God or their relationship with Him? When we identify such an idol in our lives, how should we respond?
3. (In small same-sex groups) In what area of your life do you most need God to show up in His awesomeness and why? Ask each person, "How may we pray for you?" Then have someone pray.

Preview Statements for This Week's Study

- God has two arms. One arm is mighty and powerful, demanding holiness and righteousness. One arm tenderly cares for the weak and wounded. Almighty and tender … one awesome God.
- The whole earth is Your creation. God, You are awesome!
- The nations are insignificant. God, You are awesome!
- Rulers are nothing and meaningless. God, You are awesome!
- Idols are a cheap substitute. God, You are awesome!
- Looking for some wisdom? God, You are awesome!
- God is wholly beyond us and completely above us. He is completely not like us. He is bigger and more powerful and more awesome than we can ever imagine.
- In spite of God's mighty transcendence, He is very near to each one of us.
- Even in trials, God is awesome!
- Strength for the weary. God, You are awesome!

Snapshot Summary
The most eloquent mouth could never express and the most intelligent mind cannot comprehend how incredibly awesome God is!

My Goal for You
I want you to understand some of the dimensions of God's awesomeness and be so gripped by Him that you worship Him and spend time with Him.

Key Verse to Memorize
Deuteronomy 10:17—" 'The LORD your God is the God of gods and the Lord of lords, the great, the mighty, and the awesome God.' "

(Message Notes blanks: awesome, justice, circle, idols, resources, small)

This Week's Mountaintop in Isaiah—Isaiah 40 (Selected Verses)

[10] Behold, the Lord GOD will come with might, with His arm ruling for Him. Behold, His reward is with Him and His recompense before Him.
[11] Like a shepherd He will tend His flock, in His arm He will gather the lambs and carry them in His bosom; He will gently lead the nursing ewes.

[21] Do you not know? Have you not heard? Has it not been declared to you from the beginning? Have you not understood from the foundations of the earth?
[22] It is He who sits above the circle of the earth, and its inhabitants are like grasshoppers, who stretches out the heavens like a curtain and spreads them out like a tent to dwell in.
[26] Lift up your eyes on high and see who has created these stars, the One who leads forth their host by number, He calls them all by name; because of the greatness of His might and the strength of His power, not one of them is missing.

It Happened to Me

On February 3, 1988, our second son, Landon, was born. Though he was rather "blue" as he entered this world, the hospital staff quickly got him breathing and crying, and we wept for joy at the sight of our second son. After all the excitement, I went home to get some sleep.

Imagine my shock to return to the hospital and find my wife sitting on the bed wiping away a quiet stream of tears.

"They have taken Landon to Lutheran General's neonatal intensive care unit. He was turning blue and couldn't breathe; they are going to find the problem and do what they can."

As the minutes turned to hours, the diagnosis was firm and grim. Diaphramatic hernia! A rare condition where the diaphragm doesn't close and keep the intestines below the stomach. Floating upward during gestation, the intestines force the heart to the right of the chest and compress the lungs in such a way that they cannot properly form. Landon's X-rays showed his left lung was almost nonexistent and his right lung was far below capacity.

Eighty-eight percent of children born with this condition do not survive the first 24 hours. We struggled to accept the nurses' near-verdict that he "might not live through the night." Moments later, we sat in our car outside the hospital with empty arms and heads bowed in trembling prayer to an awesome God.

"Lord, we do not understand why this is happening. We bring our fears and heartache to You. We want You to accomplish something for our new son that is so far beyond us we can only turn in faith to You. We are asking for You to heal him. Use the doctors, use the medication, use what You will, but cause his organs to be realigned and his lungs to be re-formed and he will belong to You, for Your purposes and for Your plans. If this is not Your will, help us accept what You have planned."

As I closed my prayer, we both experienced what we had only heard reported, God's incredible peace that "surpasses all understanding" (Phil. 4:7).

The next morning I was buoyed to know that the good people of our church, along with countless family and friends, were holding us up and asking God for a miracle. Landon struggled through the night, striving for every breath. Before the sun was up, his little chest was opened wide and his intestine tucked back below his stomach. The diaphragm was sewn shut to hold it all in place and they closed his chest with heart and lungs still misplaced, knowing he could handle no more.

We arrived at the hospital to all this news and the critical need for more prayer that his limited lungs would give enough air to sustain life for a second surgery and protect him from brain damage. The next three days were agonizing. But alongside the stress was an outpouring of prayer like we had never known. Every nurse and doctor must have known of our faith as they witnessed the steady stream of phone calls and visitors and saw us time and again huddled and holding hands around our son, calling out to our awesome God.

By the fifth day, Landon was strong enough to face the second surgery. I was standing beside Dr. Jae as he saw the X-ray for the first time. He strained to comprehend what he was seeing. Confirming that it was in fact the X-ray of our son, he puzzled a moment more and then turned to the intern standing with me.

"What's wrong with this patient?" he barked in an almost angry tone.

The intern looked at the X-ray and reluctantly admitted, "I don't know."

The X-ray revealed that his displaced heart was in its rightful place. A miracle, beyond description and irrefutable. Landon's left lung was rightly placed and full of the squiggly X-ray lines that revealed a nourishing flow of air. Another miracle.

The few babies who survive this birth defect spend weeks or months in the NICU, but Landon was home by the end of the seventh day. An irrefutable miracle from an awesome God.

Months later, a friend of ours heard our doctor speak at a medical colloquium. When asked about the unexplainable in the field of medicine, Dr. Jae reluctantly told the story of Landon's healing, admitting that sometimes "medicine meets marvels that defy explanation." A human description of an awesome God.

As I write this, we're planning Landon's 17th birthday celebration. How do I know that God is awesome? It happened to me!

DAY ONE *Get a Grip on God's Awesomeness*

🍃 **Read Today's Walk in the Word verse in the margin, meditate on God's name, and talk to the Lord in prayer as you begin today's study.**

① **I want to invite you to memorize Deuteronomy 10:17 (Today's Walk in the Word). Begin memorizing it and fill in the blanks below.**

"The Lord your _____ is the _____ of gods and the _____ of

lords, the _____, the _____, and the _____ God."

Only God Is Really Awesome!

Most of us get the idea, we just don't have a clue about the magnitude of His awesomeness. When we call something awesome these days, we mean "cool" or "wow" or "what an upgrade!" Awesome is our label for everything superlative.

• "Mom, these cookies are awesome."

• "Awesome job on that project!"

• "Check out my boom box. The sub woofers are awesome!"

Then we come to church and sing, "Our God is an awesome God," and wonder why our worship falls flat. We've ruined another word. God is awesome indeed, but our flippant use of the term has made it as interesting as vanilla. At best, a cliche. Only when we encounter the One who is truly awesome—only then are we speechless.

Maybe speechless is the best way to approach God's awesomeness. Everything that is God is awesome and everything that is awesome is God. At my house, you're not allowed to use the word *awesome* for anyone or anything except God. It's the rule … because it's the truth. To call anything else awesome is a joke. Real awesomeness can send shivers up your spine. At the risk of sounding simplistic, *awesome* means "producing awe."

There are, however, two sides of awesome. One side is fearful, dreadful, scary, even terrifying. Hebrews 10:31 says it right, "It is a terrifying thing to fall into the hands of the living God." But the flip side is that when you are gripped by God's greatness, His awesomeness runs like a river of joy through the very center of your being. You know beyond any doubt that you were created for Him, for this moment. God's awesomeness takes you to your knees in total reverence, to worship without self-consciousness and to walk in glad surrender.

Today's Walk in the Word
Deuteronomy 10:17—" 'The LORD your God is the God of gods and the Lord of lords, the great, the mighty, and the awesome God.' "

Meditate on God's Name
The great, the mighty, and the awesome God (Deuteronomy 10:17)

Talk to the Lord
Great, mighty, and awesome God, even Your name is beyond my understanding. You are great, yet You allow me access to talk to You! You are mighty—Almighty. And I surely need Your mighty arm and hand to work in my behalf. You are awesome. I am awed at who You are and all You have made. Lord, as I study this week, expand my capacity to grasp something more of Your greatness. Enable me to stand in genuine awe of You. Amen.

AWESOME
producing awe, amazing

② **Below are some synonyms (similar words) and some antonyms (opposite words) of awesome. Check all the antonyms of awesome.**

- ❑ astonishing
- ❑ blah
- ❑ awe-inspiring
- ❑ breathtaking
- ❑ ho-hum
- ❑ dreadful
- ❑ grand
- ❑ wonderful

- ❑ fearful
- ❑ daunting
- ❑ ordinary
- ❑ formidable
- ❑ impressive
- ❑ exalted
- ❑ overwhelming
- ❑ lackluster

- ❑ trivial
- ❑ unimpressive
- ❑ mind-blowing
- ❑ magnificent
- ❑ lame
- ❑ far out
- ❑ striking
- ❑ dull

Antonyms of Awesome
blah, ho-hum, ordinary, lackluster, trivial, unimpressive, lame, dull

Synonyms of Awesome
astonishing, awe-inspiring, breathtaking, dreadful, grand, wonderful, fearful, daunting, formidable, impressive, exalted, overwhelming, mind-blowing, magnificent, far out, striking

③ **Using some of the synonyms in the margin, write your own definition of awesome.**

_____

_____

Psalm 91:1—*"He who dwells in the shelter of the Most High Will abide in the shadow of the Almighty."*

God's Awesomeness—Your Shelter

In the Bible, God's awesomeness and His name, Almighty, often go together. God Almighty is translated El-Shaddai in Hebrew, which literally means "God of the mountains." Every time you read about God Almighty think of His mountain-like majesty in whose presence there is a "secret place" or a shadow. In His awesomeness, you can find shelter. When the psalmist needed protection in times of need, he went to God, his awesome mountain of safety. You, too, have this place of refuge in God's awesomeness. You may want to memorize Psalm 91:1 so you know where to run when you need shelter: "He who dwells in the shelter of the Most High will abide in the shadow of the Almighty."

④ **What name of God can remind you of His shelter and protection in a time of need?**

_____

Clear the Way for God to Work

Isaiah knew all about God's awesomeness. He proclaimed it without apology to an apathetic and aggressively wicked audience. Within the limitations of language, the Holy Spirit gave Isaiah the greatest description of God's awesomeness ever penned. His words are God's words about Himself, and they are worthy of our careful study. Our Scripture focus this week takes us to Isaiah 40.

We each have obstacles in our lives that hinder us from hearing God's word. That's why Isaiah begins chapter 40 with " 'Clear the way for the LORD in the wilderness; make smooth in the desert a highway for our God' " (v. 3). When it comes to communicating with His people, God wants nothing to hinder His truth from reaching us. He wants every obstacle out of the way.

⑤ Read Isaiah 40:3-5 in the margin and think about obstacles that may be blocking God's access to your life. Check any that apply. Then pray about what you need to do to remove these obstacles. Write notes below or on a separate sheet of paper.

❏ any voids or areas of deficiency or need (valley) that need to be filled?

❏ any problems or barriers (mountains and hills) that need to be brought down or made low?

❏ any broken relationships that make the way rough and need to be smoothed out?

❏ any crooked or wicked way, any twisted behavior that needs to be straightened out?

❏ any sin or unholy behavior that keeps you separated from fellowship with God?

_____

_____

_____

_____

Isaiah 40:3-5—

"A voice is calling,
'Clear the way for the LORD
in the wilderness;
Make smooth in the desert
a highway for our God.
'Let every valley be lifted up,
And every mountain and hill
be made low;
And let the rough ground
become a plain,
And the rugged terrain
a broad valley;
Then the glory of the LORD
will be revealed,
And all flesh will see it together.' "

What's blocking His access to your life? Could it be you? Get out of His way! Perhaps other people are hindering His truth from reaching you. I challenge you to stand still in the importance of this moment and let God's awesome power and presence transform your perspective.

In these beginning verses of chapter 40, Isaiah tells of another voice that says, "Call out." And we would then ask, " 'What shall I call out?' " How could we possibly find words to describe an awesome God to our generation? Isaiah said, "The grass withers, the flower fades, but the word of our God stands forever" (v. 8). Our words are like grass—they dry up and blow away. But God's Word endures forever. This week, let's dive into what God says about Himself in the Bible.

Isaiah 40:8—

"The grass withers,
the flower fades,
But the word of our God
stands forever."

🌿 **Pause to pray.** Ask God to help you remove any obstacles that are blocking God's access to your life. Invite God to grip you with His awesomeness this week.

DAY TWO *Awesome Creator*

Read Today's Walk in the Word verses in the margin and on the next page, meditate on God's name, and talk to the Lord in prayer as you begin today's study.

Today's Walk in the Word
Isaiah 40:10-11—
*"Behold, the Lord GOD will come
    with might,
With His arm ruling for Him.
Behold, His reward is with Him
And His recompense before Him.
Like a shepherd He will tend
    His flock,
In His arm He will gather
    the lambs
And carry them in His bosom."*

Meditate on God's Name
The Creator of the ends
of the earth (Isaiah 40:28)

Talk to the Lord
My Creator, I am amazed at the
beauty and complexity of Your
handiwork. It's breathtaking! I
do stand in awe of You. Today, I
worship You. Amen.

Review Your Memory Verse
Deuteronomy 10:17—" *'The LORD
your God is the God of gods and
the Lord of lords, the great, the
mighty, and the awesome God.' "*

Example:
My God is a gentle Shepherd.
I'm comforted when He carries
    me in His arms.

Which God Do You Know?

Isaiah begins his description of God with what sounds like a contradiction. Most people know either the God of verse 10 or the God of verse 11. Both are true. Both are powerful! In his first description, Isaiah writes:

> Behold, the Lord GOD will come with might,
> With His arm ruling for Him.
> Behold, His reward is with Him
> And His recompense [justice] before Him (Isa. 40:10).

Have you experienced that strong arm of God? Good! But if that's all you know, then be gripped by His other arm described in verse 11:

> Like a shepherd He will tend His flock,
> In His arm He will gather the lambs
> And carry them in His bosom;
> He will gently lead the nursing ewes (Isa. 40:11).

God is a shepherd, scooping up His lambs and carrying them close to Him. God provides special treatment for special needs. At certain times your Shepherd will say, "This one is hurting. Careful of her wound. We're going to have to carry her for a while." This tender arm of God reminds us of His unique and personal care for us.

① **With which side of God's nature are you most familiar?**
❑ a. the mighty, powerful, and strong God (v. 10)
❑ b. the tender, gentle, caring Shepherd (v. 11)

God has two arms. One arm is mighty and powerful, demanding holiness and righteousness. One arm tenderly cares for the weak and wounded. Almighty and tender … one awesome God.

② **Write a two-line psalm of your own, praising God for His mighty power and/or His tender care. I've included an example in the margin.**

_____

_____

The Whole Earth Is Your Creation. God, You Are Awesome!

Take a good look at your hand. Hold it out. Inspect your fingers and your palms. Pretty useful tools, aren't they? Maybe that's why Isaiah uses them to describe creation. He tells us that God is One "who has measured the waters in the hollow of His hand, and marked off the heavens by the span" (v. 12).

"Measured the waters." Cup your hand. Look at that little place down there in the middle. Think about all of the water in all the world—God measured the oceans from the hollow of His hand. To be a little more exact, that's 322,280,000 cubic miles of water. That's a mile by a mile by a mile, 322,280,000 times. And God's saying, "Got it right here in My palm."

"Marked off the heavens by the span." The span of your hand is the distance from the tip of your thumb to the tip of your little finger when the hand is fully extended. In biblical days, a hand's span was a common measuring tool. I can almost get my span around an orange. You try it. You've seen Shaquille O'Neal on the basketball court, right? He could probably get his span around half a basketball. God, on the other hand, can palm the world. God says, "See the earth? It's 24,830 miles all the way around—got it right here in My palm!"

And it's only because of His mercy and patience that He doesn't slam dunk us all. Doesn't that blow you away?

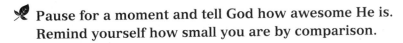 Pause for a moment and tell God how awesome He is. Remind yourself how small you are by comparison.

Next Isaiah tells us that God "calculated the dust of the earth by the measure" (v. 12). Ever try to move the dirt around in your backyard? Our awesome God laid down all the soil on the whole planet.

Notice also the direct involvement of God in creation; He is calculating, measuring, spanning. Those who would say that somehow God began some evolutionary process and then withdrew haven't understood Isaiah 40. Clearly, God spoke the world into existence. He was personally the agency and the instrumentality of its creation. God did it. He is "The Creator"!

With all my heart I believe God did all this in 6 literal 24-hour days. I'm not troubled by scientific skeptics who think they know more than what God's Word says. The historians, geologists, and evolutionary scientists of the world have often challenged the Bible only to be proven wrong. It's almost laughable to think of them trying to figure out God's program. I'm going to stick with what God has said in the matters yet to be verified by science. I'm sure He's not holding His breath waiting to be validated.

Notice God's majesty in the next phrase. "And [He] weighed the mountains in a balance, and the hills in a pair of scales." Picture the mountainscapes of the world. God said, "O.K. Put the Rockies on this side of the scale. Bring them up into Canada. Now let's make the Himalayas. How big do we want those?"

Isn't that awesome? Doesn't that make you feel tiny? Let's jump down to verse 21. I love Isaiah's attitude here.

> Do you not know? Have you not heard?
> Has it not been declared to you from the beginning?
> Have you not understood from the foundations of the earth?
> It is He who sits above the circle of the earth,
> And its inhabitants are like grasshoppers,
> Who stretches out the heavens like a curtain
> And spreads them out like a tent to dwell in (Isa. 40:21-22).

If you feel small when you imagine God's creation, it's because you are! God says we're like grasshoppers! Picture yourself on a hot summer night out on the deck with your family and friends having a barbecue. How much do the grasshoppers in your lawn affect your evening? A little background noise maybe? Hardly a distraction. That's the entire human race before God and His awesome purposes.

Now look at verse 22. "It is He who sits above the circle of the earth." Twenty-two hundred years before Christopher Columbus, God said our planet was circular and not flat. Here it was in God's Word all along. Ditto on the science versus Scripture comment above. I'll go with God's explanation every time.

③ **Read through the words in the margin and circle three that best describe what you are thinking about God at this moment.**

④ **Words aren't big enough, are they? Write three words that describe what you are thinking about yourself in comparison to your Creator.**

_____ _____ _____

The Heavens Are Your Handiwork. God, You Are Awesome!
But God "stretches out the heavens like a curtain and spreads them out like a tent to dwell in" (v. 22). The word *heavens* describes all of God's created universe. He said, "Now, let's make the universe" and poof … as easily as you put up an umbrella, it was all there. Do you have any idea the immensity of the universe God spoke into existence? I've tried for many years to find a decent description. Try this on for size: We're on planet earth, and we are 93,000,000 miles from the sun. Imagine that distance as the thickness of a piece of paper. From the earth to the sun, 93 million miles equals a piece of paper.

With that in mind, the distance to the nearest star is a stack of paper 71 feet high, with every single piece of paper representing 93 million miles. (Stay with me; this is getting outrageous.) The size of our galaxy is represented by a stack of paper 310 miles high (the distance from Chicago to St. Louis), with every single piece of paper in that stack representing 93 million miles. That's just our galaxy, and it's one among millions.

You say, "Oh, I understand that." Well, think about this then.

- mighty
- grand
- majestic
- stupendous
- huge
- great
- awesome
- colossal
- enormous
- fantastic
- phenomenal
- gigantic
- monumental
- staggering
- dynamite
- stunning
- breathtaking
- mind-boggling
- gargantuan
- humongous
- immense
- immeasurable
- infinite
- measureless
- limitless
- unbounded
- vast
- multitudinous

The known universe is a stack of paper 31 million miles high with every piece of paper representing 93 million miles! Now for those of you who like math, there are 10.4 million sheets of paper in a stack 1 mile high. Therefore the known universe is 31 million miles of paper, with each mile representing 10.4 million sheets of paper and each sheet of paper representing 93 million miles. Are you getting a headache?

In every description we see of God's reality, we are struck by the immense distance that exists between us and God—in power, in size, in ability, in majesty. The gap is too great to measure. This must be what the astronauts felt viewing the earth from the moon's surface. We are so small … so infinitesimally tiny. God, on the other hand, could inhale the universe in a single breath. The writer of Hebrews understood this.

> You, LORD, in the beginning laid the foundation of the earth,
> And the heavens are the works of Your hands;
> They will perish, but You remain;
> And they all will become old like a garment,
> And like a mantle You will roll them up;
> Like a garment they will also be changed.
> But You are the same,
> And Your years will not come to an end (Heb. 1:10-11).

God can roll up and toss away the universe as easy as rolling up an old shirt. The immensity of it all is so much more than we can grasp.

⑤ **Fill in the blank: That's why we reserve the word _____ just for Him.**

⑥ **He alone is awesome! Just for fun, log on to the Internet (*http://hubblesite.org/*) and take a look at the pictures made by the Hubble Space Telescope. Look at the planets, the stars, the galaxies, the nebulae and be amazed at our AWESOME God who spoke it all into existence. Pick out your favorite and save it on your computer as wallpaper or a screen saver. Or make a slide show to share with your family or your small group.**

⑦ **As you think about God's creation: the heavens, the earth, the processes of life and nature, and every living thing, what most fills you with awe for your Creator?**

_____

🖉 **Close today's study in prayer. Read or sing "How Great Thou Art" as a prayer to your awesome God. Describe to Him other reasons you know He is awesome.**

NOTE: On Day 5 I recommend that you schedule a date with your Creator, but I want you to do it before your next small-group meeting if possible. Turn to page 51, read activity 2, and work it into your schedule this week.

How Great Thou Art
"O Lord my God!
    When I in awesome wonder
Consider all the worlds
    thy hands have made,
I see the stars, I hear the
    rolling thunder,
Thy pow'r thro'out the
    universe displayed,
Then sings my soul,
    my Savior God to thee;
How great thou art,
    how great thou art!
Then sings my soul,
    my Savior God to thee;
How great thou art,
    how great thou art!"[1]

Today's Walk in the Word
Psalm 33:8—
"Let all the earth fear the LORD;
Let all the inhabitants of the
world stand in awe of Him."

Meditate on God's Name
Ruler over all the kingdoms of
the nations (2 Chronicles 20:6)

Talk to the Lord
Lord and Master, Ruler over
all the earth, I stand in awe of
You. I love You, but I'm also
learning to have a reverent fear
of You. I tremble in Your holy
and awesome presence. Today, I
submit to You as my Ruler. Rule
over all my life. Amen.

Review Your Memory Verse
Deuteronomy 10:17—" 'The LORD
your God is the God of gods and
the Lord of lords, the great, the
mighty, and the awesome God.' "

🌿 **Read Today's Walk in the Word verse in the margin, meditate on God's name, and talk to the Lord in prayer as you begin today's study.**

The Nations Are Insignificant. God, You Are Awesome!
A drop in the bucket—you've heard that expression. It means almost nothing, like $100 to the national economy. That's what God thinks about the nations who disregard His awesomeness. Of course there are many people who don't give a rip about God's Word or His invitation of grace. Did you ever wonder what God thinks about them?

> Behold, the nations are like a drop from a bucket, …
> a speck of dust on the scales; …
> All the nations are as nothing before Him,
> They are regarded by Him as less than nothing
>   and meaningless (Isa. 40:15,17).

① **List five or six of the largest, most powerful nations on earth.**

_____

_____

② **Add them all together and who is greater? Check one.**
❑ a. All the mighty nations combined
❑ b. Our awesome God

Isaiah continues: "To whom then will you liken God? Or what likeness will you compare with Him?" (Isa. 40:18). Isaiah is beginning to stutter as he tries to think of words to shatter man's tiny perception of God. He's not like this … and He's so much bigger than that … and so far beyond … Then to what can we compare Him? How can we describe how awesome He truly is? We have no words.

Rulers Are Nothing and Meaningless. God, You Are Awesome!
Worried about world powers? World War III? Terrorists? Market crashes? Biological warfare? Understand this: "[God] reduces rulers to nothing," and He regards them as less than nothing and "meaningless" (Isa. 40:23).

Whatever happened to Napoleon? Didn't he die in exile on an island somewhere? Or Alexander, the not so Great? Hitler? They're dead. Or the maniac leaders of our generation such as Osama bin Laden? Their influence is hardly a blip on God's monitor. They may cause us to bite our nails and worry, but God isn't pacing or wringing

His hands. Just as soon as He's ready, He will reduce those leaders to nothing. Isaiah says in effect, "Don't you get it? God doesn't read the *New York Times*. And if He did, it wouldn't make any difference. Nothing stops God's unalterable purposes in this world!"

I can't wait for that day in heaven when we get to hear history's real story—when we read God's script and realize all He was doing behind the scenes. Just imagine the drama of God's continuous all-wise intervention in the sinful machinations of human armies and governments. To think that not one of His purposes is ever delayed or frustrated—not even for a moment. We will be amazed, stunned, and captured by God's awesome control of human affairs. When will we embrace the reality of God's awesome control over history? History is and always has been God's ball game. He decides who pitches, who scores, and who gets on base. He calls one man out and advances another runner. Awesome!

③ **Name two political realities that are insignificant and meaningless in comparison to our awesome God. Fill in the blanks.**

1. The _____ of the world are insignificant by comparison.

2. The _____ of the nations are nothing by comparison.

Idols Are a Cheap Substitute. ... God, You Are Awesome!
Nations and rulers are insignificant and meaningless in comparison to God. I think this section in Isaiah 40 on idols is the funniest part of the whole chapter. Man thinks, I can't control God. I can't understand God. I'm just going to make my own god. So Isaiah deals with that whole idol thing once and for all.

④ **Read Isaiah 40:19-20 in the margin and circle the words that describe what idols are made of. <u>Underline</u> the people who make them.**

Can you imagine some guy calling his wife from work, "Hey, Martha. I'm going to be home a little late tonight, I have to make a god." But he's not making just any god—a goldsmith puts gold over it, and a silversmith adds silver chains.

Isaiah's sarcasm in verse 20 makes me laugh. The tongue-in-cheek description is obvious. "If you can't afford a gilded god, then send today for a god made out of heavenly mahogany carved by the kingdom's most skillful craftsmen. Don't delay! This holy knick-knack is guaranteed not to wobble or fall down. Get yours today for $39.95." Do you see how ludicrous that is?

Careful! Don't miss the application for each of us. Idols are not just in Isaiah's day nor are they only in the dark African jungles. We've polished our image a bit, but idols still serve as a cheap substitute for God.

Isaiah 40:19-20—
"As for the idol, a craftsman casts it,
A goldsmith plates it with gold,
And a silversmith fashions chains of silver.
He who is too impoverished for such an offering
Selects a tree that does not rot;
He seeks out for himself a skillful craftsman
To prepare an idol that will not totter."

⑤ **Which of the following can be an idol, false god, or substitute for God? Check all that apply.**

❏ career, job
❏ my company, business
❏ Mohammed
❏ sports, recreational activities
❏ cars, boats, electronics
❏ education, degrees
❏ spouse, children, family
❏ house, property

❏ Buddha
❏ bank account, money, stocks
❏ hobbies, collections
❏ travel
❏ a charismatic leader
❏ computer, Internet
❏ Krishna
❏ Mother Mary

⑥ **What other things or people can you think of that can become idols or false gods? List them below.**

_____

_____

_____

IDOLATER

one who worships an image or a false god.

Baal figurine

In our foolishness, we build our lives around our self-made gods. Any of the items listed above can become a false god or substitute for our relationship with God. Loving any one, any activity, or any thing too much can make you a practicing idolater.

It's time we let God be God as He has revealed Himself in His Word! That means embracing everything God says about Himself rather than making Him what we want Him to be—that is, crafting our own little idol. We can't make Scripture an *a la carte* menu. "I'll take a generous portion of the comforting, fatherly God as my main God, with a little lovey-dovey, man-upstairs God on the side, but hold the judging, holy God. Last time I had Him I had trouble sleeping!" Why would we settle for some sugary dinner-mint religion when we can have an eight-course meal of the only God who is?

🍃 **Conclude today's study in prayer to your awesome God. If you have been convicted about an idol or false god in your life, agree with God about how wrong you've been and repent! Do you need to throw away anything? Do it. Tell God how awesome He is. Mention to Him some of the things He is more awesome than: "God, you are more awesome than …"**

DAY FOUR *Awesome Compassion*

🌿 Read Today's Walk in the Word verses in the margin, meditate on God's name, and talk to the Lord in prayer as you begin today's study.

① Review your memory verse from Deuteronomy 10:17. Can you recite it from memory or write it from memory?

Looking for Some Wisdom? God, You Are Awesome!

If there was one thing I could ask for and receive each time I faced a problem, it would be God's wisdom. Like you, I long to know the wisest response, the best direction, the perfect choice in every circumstance I face. As I seek the Lord in prayer, I am reminded He's got it all figured out. Always has. Always will. He invites us to ask Him for wisdom: "If any of you lacks wisdom, let him ask of God, who gives to all generously and without reproach, and it will be given to him" (Jas. 1:5).

🌿 Why not do that now? List some of the areas, situations, or decisions for which you need the Lord's wisdom. Then ask!

_____

_____

— ⚬⚬⚬ —

Isaiah asks, "Who has directed the Spirit of the Lord or as His counselor has informed Him?" (Isa. 40:13). That's a rhetorical question if there ever was one. God has never been informed or taught about anything. God has never said, "You're kidding Me!" No one has ever given God an angle on any subject or taken Him aside for a verbal upgrade. Not once!

② Let's play a game. I'll ask the rhetorical questions from verse 14, and you give the answer.

1. With whom did God consult? _____

2. Who gave Him understanding? _____

3. Who taught Him in the path of justice? _____

4. Who taught Him knowledge? _____

5. Who informed Him of the way of understanding? _____

Today's Walk in the Word
Psalm 111:9-10— *"He has sent redemption to His people; He has ordained His covenant forever; Holy and awesome is His name. The fear of the LORD is the beginning of wisdom; A good understanding have all those who do His commandments; His praise endures forever."*

Meditate on God's Name
Our God, the great, the mighty, and the awesome God, who keeps covenant and lovingkindness (Nehemiah 9:32)

Talk to the Lord
Awesome, awesome, awesome God, You are holy, mighty, and filled with love. Teach me to fear You. I need wisdom. Help me obey You. I need understanding. I praise You. Your praise endures forever. Amen.

Review Your Memory Verse
Deuteronomy 10:17—" 'The LORD your God is the God of gods and the Lord of lords, the great, the mighty, and the awesome God.' "

Isaiah 40:14—*"With whom did He consult and who gave Him understanding? And who taught Him in the path of justice and taught Him knowledge And informed Him of the way of understanding?"*

Did you get the pattern? No one influences God. No one impacts the Lord. No one changes His mind about anything. He doesn't need you, me, or anyone to teach Him anything. When we hear that, our natural response is, "Don't I matter at all to God?" That's not the point. The point is that God loves you and me because He chooses to do so.

Get rid of the twisted thinking that God loves you because He saw something in you that attracted Him. That may be the way human relationships work. "God cares for me because I am a hard worker or a caring neighbor or a faithful parent." Wrong! He loves you because He chooses to do so.

At first that's hard to take. "I want God to care for me because He really likes me." But if God only loves us because of who we are, then we have to lie to ourselves about who we are in order to receive that care. He doesn't love you any more or any less because of who you are or what you do. He loves you to the max simply because in His mercy He chose to do so. His nature is love.

Do you see how freeing that is? Any risk you have of losing God's love goes out the window. You can never be outside His circle of love because it's not about you—it's about Him.

Bigger Than I Imagine and Nearer Than I Think

There is one last and very important truth about God's awesomeness. Again, it has two parts—both critical to understand.

On one side is God's transcendence. It's what we've been covering throughout this chapter. God is wholly beyond us and completely above us. He is completely not like us. He is bigger and more powerful and more awesome than we can ever imagine. No one can see God and live, "for our God is a consuming fire" (Heb. 12:29).

TRANSCENDENCE
state of being above and beyond and higher than the experience of our senses

③ **What is one aspect of God's awesomeness describing how far above and beyond us He is?**

He is _____

If God's awesomeness was only seen in His transcendence, then we would have no relationship with Him. How can you know and fellowship with the powerful and completely independent God of the universe? We could not fellowship with Him apart from His equally awesome imminence. Imminence is like the little sticker on the passenger side mirror of your car that says, "Objects in this mirror are closer than they appear." The Bible teaches that in spite of God's mighty transcendence, He is very near to each one of us.

IMMINENCE
state of being close, near

④ **What is a second aspect of God's awesomeness that describes His nearness? God's** _____

I am thankful for the comfort of God's nearness, but it breaks my heart to hear His imminence preached in so many churches to the exclusion of His awesome transcendence. Then we end up with a little God who might be imminent (i.e., close), but totally impotent. So let's get these two truths into alignment with each other and in our own hearts. Like two towers that can never be toppled, God is both imminent and transcendent. Ominous … and near. Out of this world … yet as close as your next breath.

⑤ **Match God's trait on the left with the correct definitions on the right. Write each letter beside a number.**

___ ___ 1. Imminent

___ ___ 2. Transcendent

a. Near, close
b. Distant, different, above
c. He's huge, far beyond what I can comprehend.
d. I can know Him and relate to Him.

Even in Trials, God Is Awesome!

In view of God's compassionate, attentive imminence, Isaiah insists that the people stop saying, "My way is hidden from the LORD, and the justice due me escapes the notice of my God" (Isa. 40:27). Isaiah is thinking, "Time out! Everybody knock off the whining and saying dumb stuff that isn't even true." I know you may feel like God has forgotten you. I realize circumstances may even lead you to doubt Him—but God has not forgotten you, and you must believe that. (The answers to activity 5 are 1-a,d; 2-b,c.)

⑥ **Have you ever felt as though God had forgotten you? Are you there right now?**
❑ a. Yes, I've been there before; but, thank God, I'm not there now.
❑ b. No, I can't think of a time when I ever felt distant or forgotten.
❑ c. That's me … right now! Where are you, Lord?

It's good to remember at this point that Isaiah was writing to a people who had just been told they were going to suffer incredible persecution as a discipline from God. What was their crime? They forgot who God was. They lost all sense of proportion regarding God's greatness. God's presence demanded awe, and they yawned. For multiple generations they had rebelliously, willfully, happily done their own thing, even worshiped other gods—and God said, "Enough!"

Isaiah's audience cried out for the Lord. They asked, "Where is He when we need Him?" Isaiah is saying, "He's right where you left Him. He hasn't moved an inch."

Like Isaiah's original audience, we live in decadent (or morally corrupt) days among a people who have disdained and diluted the biblical concepts of God. Let Isaiah's message of God's awesome nature blow across your parched heart and bring refreshment to your soul.

God said through Isaiah, "Tell them hard times are coming, but don't give up—now or ever. Don't underestimate My power to reorder the universe. Tell them to keep trusting Me and living the way I told them to in spite of what's coming."

> Let Isaiah's message of God's awesome nature blow across your parched heart and bring refreshment to your soul.

How can they? How can you or I? By getting a grip on God's awesomeness. In Isaiah 49:15-16 God says,

" 'Can a woman forget her nursing child,
And have no compassion on the son of her womb?
Even these may forget, but I will not forget you.
"Behold, I have inscribed you on the palms of My hands.' "

⑦ **Imagine Jesus standing in heaven praying for you. He looks at His nail-scarred hands and says, "Don't worry. I cannot forget you." Draw a simple picture of Jesus and/or His hands in the margin. Thank Him for caring that much for you.**

Strength for the Weary. God You Are Awesome!

I love what Isaiah says next. "Do you not know? Have you not heard? The Everlasting God, the LORD, the Creator of the ends of the earth does not become weary or tired" (Isa. 40:28). He's not like us. He never gets tired. He never feels overwhelmed.

"His understanding is inscrutable" (v. 28). How great would God be if average intellects like yours and mine ever got a total handle on who He is?

When your battery is running low, God knows it! "He gives strength to the weary and to him who lacks might He increases power" (v. 29). Some people might say, "I don't really need God's strength. I have my own program." You are so wrong!

As a pastor I often interact with people who boast, "I have my act together. I have a career plan, my education, and I'm heading in a good direction. My future's bright." Listen, please. Surrender your pride before God brings you low. You will never break God's back, but He will break yours. You will not deny His purposes. If you don't bow your knee before Him willingly, He will force you to your knees. Believe me, you want to choose Him now.

"Though youths grow weary and tired, and vigorous young men stumble badly" (v. 30), every one needs God. Even the strongest. Even the youngest. The sooner you learn that, the less pain you will experience. You ask, "How do I get that strength?"

⑧ **Read the promise in Isaiah 40:31 in the margin and underline what you must do to gain new strength.**

You may say, "Wait? I don't have time to wait. I drive fast, eat in a hurry, talk without taking a breath—I'm living in the fast lane. Don't make me wait." Sorry! God says to wait on Him. And there's a promise if you do: new strength and endurance.

"But are God's ways worth the wait?" I can't believe you're asking that after we've spent the entire chapter detailing His awesomeness! He is worth it. We easily forget how great God is. That's why we needed this lesson. Let's not forget that the God we love and serve is an awesome God indeed!

INSCRUTABLE
difficult to fathom, explain, or understand.

Isaiah 40:31—*"Those who wait for the LORD*
Will gain new strength;
They will mount up with wings like eagles.
They will run and not get tired."

🌿 Conclude today's study in prayer and praise. If you can, obtain the lyrics to "Awesome God" or another chorus that speaks of God's awesomeness and sing (or read) them. Then name to Him ways He is an awesome God.

DAY 5 *Responding to God's Awesomeness*

🌿 Read Today's Walk in the Word verse in the margin, meditate on God's name, and talk to the Lord in prayer as you begin today's study.

Think back to a time when your soul was gripped by the awesomeness of God. I remember a time I was drifting in a quiet canoe with nothing on the wind but an orchestra of birds. I could hear the rustle of trees and see their reflection on the shimmering water. I was on a wilderness trip in northern Ontario, Canada. I was miles from anything fake or manufactured. The stuff God made was magnified in all His awesome splendor.

① When and where was the last time you stood in breathless wonder of God's creation? Were you standing on the rim of the Grand Canyon? Or dangling your feet off a mountain precipice? Were you star-gazing at a million lights? Or just watching fantastic images on the Discovery Channel? Briefly describe such a time when you were gripped by God's splendor in creation.

_____

_____

_____

② Make a date with your Creator. Sometime (before your next session if possible), get alone with the God Almighty of the universe. Go somewhere to view a wonder in His creation. Sit there (or walk around) at least a half hour (or more). Don't try to tell God anything; just be available to Him. Revel in His awesomeness. Enjoy His presence. Pay attention to the little things that show His marvelous designs. Gasp at the big

Today's Walk in the Word
Psalm 145:5-6—*"On the glorious splendor of Your majesty And on Your wonderful works, I will meditate. Men shall speak of the power of Your awesome acts, And I will tell of Your greatness"*

Meditate on God's Name
Lord, the great and awesome God (Daniel 9:4)

Talk to the Lord
Lord, I've been thinking about Your wonderful works and Your awesome acts this week. It's true. You're awesome! Create opportunities for me to tell others of Your greatness so they, too, may come to know You. Amen.

Write Your Memory Verse
Deuteronomy 10:17—

_____

_____

_____

_____

things that boggle your mind to think how He created them. Call back to your mind the great things He has done in your life. All of creation is designed to point you to Him. So, wait silently before Him and allow yourself to be captured by His greatness—lost in the wonder of His majesty and awesome power. At the end of your time, sing some of your favorite songs of worship. Sing to Him! Upon your return write a brief journal entry in the margin of where you went and what you experienced. Use extra paper if you need more space.

③ Meditate on God, your Creator. Read Psalm 8 in your Bible. You may want to memorize some or all nine verses to give to Him in worship on your next time alone with God.

④ One evening after dark, go outside to look at the stars. Isaiah directed you to do just that. Read Isaiah 40:26 in the margin.

Isaiah 40:26—
"Lift up your eyes on high
And see who has created
*   these stars,*
The One who leads forth their
*   host by number,*
He calls them all by name;
Because of the greatness
*   of His might and the strength*
*   of His power,*
Not one of them is missing."

Remember God's awesomeness every evening when you see the night sky. He knows each star by name. Because of the greatness of His might and the strength of His power, not one of them is missing. And His love and care for you is a million times greater than that. Awesome!

Facing Difficult Times?
Are you facing a difficult decision or season of your life? Get a grip on God's transcendence and imminence. With His one arm, He is able to break through any barrier, overpower any obstacle; yet with His other arm, He is tenderly caring for you as a loving Shepherd. Could anything be too hard for Him? Instead of succumbing to a natural tendency toward self-pity or defeat, allow yourself to be embraced by the arms of God. Stand confident in this trial knowing that God sees you. God can do anything; and in some mysterious way, He is working all things together for His glory and your good.

⑤ Spend some time today writing down (in the margin or on separate paper) some of the awesome things you have personally experienced or seen God do in your lifetime. These may be personal or family experiences or they may be church-related experiences. Explain why you believe the author was God. Then reaffirm your faith in God's awesomeness because of all He has done and will do for you.

Troubling News?
When the evening news troubles you with its reports of world rulers out of control and murderous, senseless conflict between nations, return to Isaiah 40 and remember nothing can be done outside of God's Almighty plan. No event in human history is outside His influence. No world ruler can change God's program. Do not fear! God Almighty is working out His awesome plan.

⑥ Name one recent news story of world events that has troubled you. Describe it below. Then thank God that He is in control.

_____

_____

⑦ Here's an exercise you can try alone or with your family or friends. God's awesomeness embraces so many of His other attributes. Invent a memory device to summarize a part of God's character. For example, awesomeness is Altogether Beyond my Comprehension (A-B-C's). Or use the letters in your family's name and select a word for each letter to remind you of God's greatness. Write one or more of your acronyms in the margin. Then use it to praise your awesome God. You may even want to paint, draw, or otherwise prepare a piece of art to hang in your home reminding you of God's awesomeness.

🍃 Close this week's study with the following prayer. Pray it slowly and thoughtfully. Personalize it and make it your own.

Awesome God, through this study You have become very large in my eyes. Your awesomeness has been magnified before me. Your transcendence is so much more than I imagined and your nearness is so much closer than I thought. You are awesome, God. Your comfort and strength are all I need.

Please give me the faith and courage to take my eyes off these challenges I face today. At times, they are all I see. They've become so big as to eclipse any view I have of You and Your power. I surrender these burdens to you now—especially _____. (Name them. God loves it when we are specific in prayer.)

Thank you for inviting me to draw near to You. I'm amazed that in Your infinite power you still want my fellowship. Increase my faith so that I grasp Your greatness as a current experience. Bring Your glory to bear upon my life so that others see Your name lifted up as never before! I praise you and adore You. I worship You, Almighty God. Amen.

---

[1] "How Great Thou Art," © Copyright 1953 S. K. Hine. Assigned to Manna Music, Inc., 34244 Brooten Road, Pacific City, OR 97135. Renewed 1981 by Manna Music, Inc. All Rights Reserved. Used by permission. (ASCAP)

GRIPPED BY THE
GREATNESS
GOD
OF

GRIPPED BY THE
SOVEREIGNTY OF
GOD

Follow the session plans in the leader's guide on page 140.

Discussion Guide on God's Awesomeness

1. What have you learned or experienced about God's awesomeness this week that has been most meaningful or life changing?
2. Turn to page 40. Share your response to activity 1. How have you experienced that side of God's nature?
3. Turn to page 46 and discuss your responses to activities 5 and 6. Of all the possible idols listed, which one do you sense is the biggest challenge or temptation for the Christians you know?

🌿 **Pause to pray that God will deliver you and those around you from the influences of modern idolatry.**

4. (p. 49, activity 5) With which trait of God are you more familiar—His imminence or His transcendence and why?
5. Turn to Day 5 beginning on page 51. Share your response to ONE of the following activities: 1, 2, 5, or 7.

DVD Message Notes on God's Sovereignty (20 minutes)

Sovereignty means that _____ God designs will happen and everything He despises will ultimately be defeated in His time.
1. God's sovereignty _____.
   • What God says will happen _____.

2. God's sovereignty _____.
   - God determines all things (Eph. 1:11).
   - Sovereignty always determines outcomes.
   - Wanting the meaningful _____ of the few, God created a world in which we are free to choose.
   - Sovereignty has determined that God will be glorified in the contrast between the way His children go through suffering and the way those who do not know Him go through _____.
   - As followers of Jesus, we live and move in _____.

Responding to the Message

1. What have you learned about the meaning of God's sovereignty?
2. How can God be sovereign and humanity have free will?
3. What are some ways you have experienced God's sovereignty or seen His sovereignty at work in the world?
4. How can God's sovereignty be a comfort to those who love Him?

Preview Statements for This Week's Study

- The term *sovereignty* means "independent from external control." The concept includes the idea of supreme authority and power or the rule of a monarch.
- *Sovereignty* means God is in control of it all.
- God is way beyond our figuring out.
- God is sovereign in world events—yesterday and today!
- God can use anyone and anything to accomplish His ultimate purposes.
- "Man proposes, but God disposes." –Thomas à Kempis
- "Can you thank Me for trusting you with this experience even if I never tell you why?"
- "No pit is so deep that God's love is not deeper still."
- I will be obedient when told.
- I will be righteous when tempted.
- I will be submissive when tried.

Snapshot Summary
God's sovereignty is first painful, then slowly powerful and only over much time seen to be profitable, if in this life at all. It is to be studied with great sensitivity for the experiences of others and deep reverence for the One who controls the outcomes of every matter in the universe.

My Goal for You
I want you to understand some of the dimensions of God's sovereignty and be so gripped by Him that you obey Him and submit to His will and purposes.

Key Verse to Memorize
Romans 8:28—*"We know that God causes all things to work together for good to those who love God, to those who are called according to His purpose."*

(Message Notes blanks: everything, demonstrated, happens, declared, worship, suffering, sovereignty)

This Week's Mountaintop in Isaiah—Isaiah 45:1-13 (Selected Verses)

[1]*Thus says the LORD to Cyrus His anointed, whom I have taken by the right hand, to subdue nations before him, and to loose the loins of kings; to open doors before him so that gates will not be shut:* [2]*"I will go before you and make the rough places smooth; I will shatter the doors of bronze and cut through their iron bars.*

[3]*I will give you the treasures of darkness and hidden wealth of secret places, so that you may know that it is I, the LORD, the God of Israel, who calls you by your name. …* [4]*I have given you a title of honor though you have not known Me.* [5]*I am the LORD, and there is no other; besides Me there is no God.*

I will gird you, though you have not known Me; [6]*That men may know from the rising to the setting of the sun that there is no one besides Me. I am the LORD, and there is no other,* [7]*The One forming light and creating darkness, causing well-being and creating calamity; I am the LORD who does all these."*

It Happened to Me

My wife, Kathy, came to know Christ at 15 years of age. She was reared by divorced parents, neither of whom had a faith during her childhood. By high school she was living with a father who was living for his only daughter and pouring all of his immense love and affection into the only human relationship that mattered to him. A laborer in the construction field, he left their home early but was always there to greet her warmly and introduce an evening of meaningful conversation and discovery. On weekends they were shopping or at the beach or visiting a museum. Each hour together was filled with wise counsel. Those who knew them well witnessed a father-daughter relationship most families only dream of.

During the spring of Kathy's 15th year, her father decided that she "needed some religion in her life." When a believing aunt was to be singing in a local evangelical church, Kathy's father took her. In God's sovereignty, this was the church I attended. I was struck with Kathy the first night I met her. Invitations to our youth group came through her cousin; and Kathy's father allowed the limited exposure, considering it a harmless effect that could be easily overcome by his own influence if she ever became truly interested in "religion."

I was in the audience a few weeks later when Kathy stood to publicly acknowledge Christ as her personal Savior and Lord. Kathy's relationship with her father struggled under the weight of Kathy's new first priority.

About a year later we started dating, and during the next five years of ups and downs rooted in her father's rejection of Kathy's faith, we fell in love and married.

Over the first seven years of our marriage, Dennis came to accept Kathy's conversion and enthusiastically returned to our lives. He even listened intently as we sought to share with him the love of Christ.

By 1990 and by God's grace, Kathy had much to be thankful for—a husband, two healthy baby boys, a newborn girl only six weeks old, and an exciting new church we started together. She had a restored relationship with her father and an eternal relationship with her heavenly Father.

In the summer of 1990, my family had just visited our parents in Canada and had even shared the gospel with a more receptive Dennis than we had previously seen. We returned home rejoicing and praying that the seeds of truth would soon sprout into personal faith in Dennis' heart.

The next week Kathy called with the tone of voice every devoted husband dreads to hear, "James, there's been an accident. Dad's dead."

We got through the funeral. I gave the gospel to the sneers of a sin-hardened crowd and stood with Kathy and our kids as the casket was lowered into the ground. We endured the ritual of his pagan friends pouring beer on the grave site. As soon as we could, we headed back to Chicago with broken hearts and a lot of questions … about God's sovereignty.

"But, Lord, he was so close." "Clearly You were ripening his heart to the gospel." "Did he cry out for salvation in his last moments?"

Weeks became months and shock became sorrow deep and wide. Questions would not yield to explanation. Comfort seemed selfish and sovereignty loomed largest of all as the only place of refuge. How well I remember the words Kathy said after many months of puzzling. "I only want what God wants. I pray Dad's in heaven. I hope, like the thief on the cross, that he cried out for mercy, but most of all I know, 'shall not the Judge of all the earth deal justly?' " (Gen. 18:25) Only God's sovereignty can bring us to the place where we bow our wounded hearts and confess, "There is a God. He sovereignly rules the universe, and He does what is right. I often do not see or understand His ways, but I choose to trust Him. Someday I will know and see that He does all things well."

Is there sorrow? Yes, but it is surrounded by sovereignty. Only faith can get you to the feet of sovereignty and only grace can keep you there.

If you are struggling to get there today, journey on. No one arrives at this destination quickly or easily. However, don't let that dissuade you. It's a place of depth and quiet rest, one only comprehended when we can say from life's deepest valleys, "It happened to me."

DAY ONE *Get a Grip on God's Sovereignty*

🍃 Read Today's Walk in the Word verse in the margin, meditate on God's name, and talk to the Lord in prayer as you begin today's study.

① I invite you to memorize Romans 8:28 (Today's Walk in the Word). Begin memorizing it and fill in the blanks below.

"We know that _____ causes _____ things to

work together for _____ to those who _____ God,

to those who are _____ according to His _____."

God's Sovereignty—A Bad Rap Lately

Let's say tragedy strikes—something big like what happened on December 26, 2004, in Southeast Asia when a powerful tsunami swept as many as 300,000 men, women, and children to their deaths. Maybe someone you love dies very suddenly, or test results indicate you're the one scheduled for the early exit. Then, before the impact of the tragedy has gone from your head to your heart, some goody-two-shoes, wanna-be theologian wraps their overly familiar arm around your shoulders and whispers words intended to comfort. Instead they cut like a knife. "God is sovereign, all He allows is for a higher good." The implication is that you should swallow hard, because in the end you'll realize the torpedo that just blew a hole in the side of your boat was for your benefit.

② Have you ever observed or experienced a person saying something intended to comfort that does just the opposite like the situation described above? If so, check statements similar to those you've heard or write another you've heard.
❏ a. This was God's will, and that's always best.
❏ b. He's in a better place now.
❏ c. God must have needed her more than you do.
❏ d. Everything will work for good in the end.
❏ e. Other: _____

I hate that! What's the devastated person supposed to think? If that's all I knew about God's sovereignty over circumstances, I would conclude: "God is good sometimes, but He's cruel other times. I guess you just can't trust Him." That is not true, but it will take me a few pages to explain. So stick with me.

Today's Walk in the Word
Romans 8:28—*"We know that God causes all things to work together for good to those who love God, to those who are called according to His purpose."*

Meditate on God's Name
Sovereign Lord (Isaiah 40:10, NIV)

Talk to the Lord
Sovereign Lord, according to Your promise, You work ALL things together for my good when I love You and respond to Your call and purpose for my life. Help me learn to love and obey You so I can experience Your best in ALL things. And help me trust You when I don't understand all You allow to come my way. Open my mind this week to understand Your sovereignty. Amen.

SOVEREIGNTY

independent from external control, supreme authority and power, rule of a monarch

God's Sovereignty Defined

The term *sovereignty* means "independent from external control." The concept includes the idea of supreme authority and power or the rule of a monarch. That means:

- God is the Ruler of all.
- God answers to no one.
- God can accomplish whatever He wants in all things.
- God sees history from beginning to end. No obstacle or adversary can hinder His plan from happening.
- God is afraid of nothing, ignorant of nothing, and needing nothing.
- God always knows what's best, and He never makes a mistake.

Sovereignty means God is in control of it all. He's over things we see and things we don't see. Stuff we understand and stuff that would blow us away if we even glimpsed it for a second. Sovereignty means it's all His. Nothing can stop from happening what He purposes. Not people, events, or time. Get it? What God plans, He delivers. What God wants, God gets—His way and His timing, on time, every time. That applies to what you're going through today and to what we are going to study in Isaiah 45.

③ **How would you summarize the meaning of God's sovereignty?**

_____

_____

④ **Which of the following has the authority to overrule God's sovereign plan or will? Check all that apply.**

- ❏ kings and queens
- ❏ national presidents
- ❏ senates and parliaments
- ❏ the pope and archbishops
- ❏ Satan and evil spirits
- ❏ me (you)
- ❏ dictators
- ❏ multinational corporate CEOs
- ❏ billionaires
- ❏ pastors and priests
- ❏ other gods
- ❏ none of the above

If you checked "none of the above" then you're on the right track. God rules over all and is in control of everyone and everything— no exceptions.

But let's face this fact: God's display of His sovereignty some-times is scary, but only because it's so not like us. Sovereignty is all about being God. In our need for control, we tend to want a God who is manageable. We reduce Him to some heavenly pal or celestial bellboy. We want to use the Lord like a rabbit's foot. Someone "lucky" to hold on to when the dam breaks and the water's rising. In some twisted way, we think we're more secure when we've got God figured out.

Sovereignty says, "No way!" There's no way you're going to figure out God. He's more than we can understand or might dare to imagine.

Here's another hard fact: When it comes to how He directs the people and events of history, God doesn't need our permission.

God doesn't need our permission.

I hate to tell you, but He's not going to stoop down and explain why He's doing everything He chooses to do. With both the macro and microscopic world under His constant control, God is able to do whatever He pleases whenever He wishes. I want you to remember this when we get to the end of the chapter, because there's something very comforting I want to share then. For now, let's agree— God is way beyond our figuring out. That's not only OK … that's the way it needs to be.

Can you imagine how small God would be if we could comprehend all that He allows and why? What if the smartest and wisest of all mankind ran the universe; can you imagine the cosmic mess we would be in? It only makes sense that an element of mystery surrounds God's person and His ways.

⑤ **Mark the following statements about God "T" for True and "F" for False.**
___ 1. God's sovereignty is limited by the permissions people give Him.
___ 2. God accomplishes what He purposes.
___ 3. If I'm smart enough and study long enough, I will be able to understand everything about God. Somebody's probably already written a book explaining everything about Him.
___ 4. God is in control of history.
___ 5. God is surrounded in mystery. I can't possibly understand everything about Him.

In the next few pages we're going to circle the base of the mountain of God's greatness, this time with His sovereignty in mind. Clouds block our view of the complete picture and even up higher when we break through the clouds, we discover we're only in the foothills. God is so much greater than us. Beside Him, we stand so infinitesimally small. Let that sink into your soul, and you'll begin to feel a surprising comfort. (The answers to activity 5 are T—2,4,5; F—1,3).

God's Sovereignty—Lord God; Sovereign Lord
Lord God. We throw God's title around like we're on a first name basis. Yet Isaiah calls God the reverential name, Adonai Yahweh or Lord God. *Adonai* speaks of God's unlimited authority. He is Master. He is Lord. *Yahweh* reminds us of His covenant relationship—the intimacy He has with His people. He is "I AM WHO I AM" (Ex. 3:14). Out of absolute reverence for God's sovereignty, Jews will not pronounce *Yahweh*, God's personal name, but substitute *Adonai* (Lord) in its place. In passages like Isaiah 40:10 where Adonai and Yahweh come together, instead of reading Lord Lord, translators render the name "Lord God" (NASB and KJV) or "Sovereign Lord" (NIV).

The God who "dwells in unapproachable light" (1 Tim. 6:16) is not to be messed with. He is larger than life. He is bigger than the universe. He is Lord, Master. But He is also Yahweh, the God of mercy and revealed love to His people.

God is way beyond our figuring out.

1 Timothy 6:15-16
"He who is the blessed and only Sovereign, the King of kings and Lord of lords, who alone possesses immortality and dwells in unapproachable light."

The call to every believer is to live with that tension—not only is He the "friend who sticks closer than a brother" (Prov. 18:24), but He is sovereign Master of the universe. "Thus says the Lord, your Redeemer, and the one who formed you from the womb, 'I, the LORD, am the maker of all things, stretching out the heavens by Myself and spreading out the earth all alone' " (Isa. 44:24).

⑥ **What name of God reveals that He is the supreme Ruler and Master of the universe?**

_____

⑦ **How should a person respond to the desires and commands of the Sovereign LORD? Check one.**
   ❏ a. Do whatever he or she (the person) wants.
   ❏ b. Completely obey the Sovereign Lord.

🍂 **Close today's study by inviting God to grip you with His sovereignty this week. Pray that He will enable you to trust Him and obey Him even when you don't understand or agree.**

DAY TWO *God's Sovereignty Explained* (A BIT)

🍂 **Read Today's Walk in the Word verses in the margin, meditate on God's name, and talk to the Lord in prayer as you begin today's study.**

As we begin our look at Isaiah 45, I want to explain to you God's sovereignty. But you already realize, don't you, that God is so great we can't possibly know and understand everything about Him?

God Is Sovereign Over History
The issue of God's sovereignty most clearly shows up in our world on the evening news. We watch the transfer of power from one nation to another, and the displacement of once "invincible" rulers—all of this is God's sovereignty at work. What about the war on terror? What about Israel's leadership? To those who think they are independent of a sovereign God, Isaiah answers, "He it is who reduces rulers to nothing, Who makes the judges of the earth meaningless. … Scarcely has their stock taken root in the earth, but He merely blows on them, and they

wither, and the storm carries them away like stubble" (Isa. 40:23-24). Yes, God is sovereign in world events—yesterday and today!

At its peak, the Babylonian Empire covered many countries in the news today: Israel, Iran, Iraq, Saudi Arabia, Syria, and Turkey. Nebuchadnezzar, the king of Babylon, invaded Jerusalem, conquered the people, and devastated the temple taking all the items of worship. In addition, he took captive the choice young men from the nation of Israel and made them court slaves.

After Nebuchadnezzar came other kings: Darius, Belshazzar, and his father, Nabonidus. You can get a firsthand account of this whole period by reading the book of Daniel; the prophet who experienced the whole thing.

Toward the end of Daniel's life came the Medo-Persian Empire. In October 539 B.C., an army led by a Persian king named Cyrus marched on Babylon and swallowed the whole empire. Before the month of October was over, Cyrus faced his captives and said in effect, "I'm the new king on the block and things are going to be different around here. I am going to be your savior and deliverer."

Cyrus released all the deported Israelites, allowing them to flee Babylon. In one day, 50 thousand Jews returned to their homeland. This is significant! If that release had not happened, it's very doubtful a nation of Israel would have existed in Christ's day, let alone in ours. All that God wanted to do in bringing the Messiah into the world hinged on this pagan king, Cyrus. Cyrus didn't love or submit to God in any way, but God used him. That's why God called Cyrus "His anointed" (Isa. 45:1).

That word *anointed* is the same word that is translated other places in the Bible as *Messiah*. God is so completely sovereign and entirely in control that when He wants to get something done, He can even use a person who hates Him to accomplish His sovereign will. Nothing can ever stop or slow God's sovereign purposes.

① **Which of the following statements is true?**
  ❑ a. Because God is sovereign, He can use anyone—including pagans—to accomplish His purposes.
  ❑ b. Even though God is sovereign, He only uses His chosen people and His followers (disciples) to carry out His plans.

God rules over history, and He knows in advance how people will respond to His purposes even if they do not know or follow Him as Lord GOD. Amazingly, 150 years before the events happened, God revealed to Isaiah the details surrounding Israel's return to the promised land. We study Isaiah 45 as history, but Isaiah spoke it as prophecy. He even gave the exact name of the ruler that God would use. I'm guessing when Cyrus showed up in Babylon, Daniel smiled with the scroll of Isaiah in His hand.

Here is how God described Cyrus: "Cyrus [My] anointed, whom I have taken by the right hand, to subdue nations" (v. 1). Cyrus might have thought he was the one conquering empires, but God says, "You're just a little boy. I was leading you by the hand."

Talk to the Lord
Whoa! Lord, can that be? I know that You love and care for me—that my well-being is Your doing. But this "calamity" part ... Do You really do that, too? Would you explain that one to me? You've got my attention! Amen.

Review Your Memory Verse
Romans 8:28—*"We know that God causes all things to work together for good to those who love God, to those who are called according to His purpose."*

God told Cyrus he was appointed to "loose the loins of kings; to open doors before him so that gates will not be shut" (v. 1). God also said:

> "I will go before you and make the rough places smooth;
> I will shatter the doors of bronze and cut through their
> iron bars.
> I will give you the treasures of darkness,
> And hidden wealth of secret places,
> So that you may know that it is I,
> The LORD, the God of Israel, who calls you by your name"
> (Isa. 45:2-3).

Interestingly, we have no indication Cyrus ever came to any kind of faith relationship with the One true God. But still, God sovereignly used him. God can use anyone and anything to accomplish His ultimate purposes.

Why did God do it? "For the sake of Jacob My servant, and Israel My chosen one," (v. 4) God says. From the first chapter of Ezra, we learn that Cyrus was so generous to the Jews he actually stormed the treasury in Babylon and gave back their golden instruments of worship which Nebuchadnezzar had taken more than a century earlier. "Not only can you go back," God is saying, "but I'm returning all the treasures stolen from you." How they must have rejoiced on the journey home to have seen God's sovereignty up close!

Isaiah 45:4-6

" 'I have also called you
   by your name;
I have given you a title of honor
Though you have not known Me.
" 'I am the LORD, and there
   is no other;
Besides Me there is no God.
I will gird you, though you have
   not known Me;
That men may know from the
   rising to the setting of the sun
That there is no one besides Me.
I am the LORD, and there
   is no other.' "

② **Read about God and His work in Cyrus in Isaiah 45:4-6 in the margin. Underline the phrases that indicate God is unique and one-of-a-kind.**

"No other," "no God," and "no one besides Me" describe our one-of-a-kind God. God is the unique Ruler of the universe. He is the King of human history. Nothing happens in this world by chance. Nothing! Forget about luck. There is no such thing as coincidence. There is only this sovereign God who rules over all that we are and do.

③ **As a reminder of God's uniqueness, draw a picture in the margin of a sunrise and/or a sunset or otherwise illustrate verse 6: "from the rising to the setting of the sun." Use colorful crayons if you like.**

While Napoleon was leading his armies over much of Europe, they won astounding victories. At one point, someone was heard to say to Napoleon, "Is God on the side of France?" In other words, "How could all of these victories be taking place but that God must be doing this." In his arrogance Napoleon said, "God is on the side that has the heaviest artillery." But then came the Battle of Waterloo where Napoleon lost both the war and his world. In very short order the entire empire collapsed.

Years later, while he was in exile on the island of St. Helena, he was reported to have quoted the words of Thomas à Kempis, "Man proposes, but God disposes."[1] We can fire up all kinds of dreams and ideas, even spend ourselves trying to see them happen. But the "end game," as they say, is all about a sovereign God. Our only real choice is whether we are for Him or against Him. And amazingly He can work His purposes regardless of the choice we make.

④ **Since you have a choice, which of the following would be the way you would most like to live your life? Check one.**
   ❑ a. I want to follow my own dreams and plans and live free from the control of anyone else—especially God.
   ❑ b. I want to know and follow God's sovereign plans. I want to live for His purposes and according to His desires.
   ❑ c. I will live according to God's plans unless I don't like His plans. Then I'll live according to my desires.

You do have a choice, but only choice *b* allows you to experience God's sovereign best in life. Resisting God's sovereign rule is rebellion against the Creator and Ruler of the universe—not a wise choice!

God Is Sovereign Over Well-Being AND Calamity

We can never completely explain the sovereignty of God, but we can share the light Scripture gives us:

⑤ **Read Isaiah 45:6-7 in the margin and underline the third line of this poetry beginning with the word "Causing."**

He is "causing well-being and creating calamity." Many people struggle with the relationship between an all-powerful God who claims to be loving yet doesn't stop suffering. In reality God does far more than fail to stop human hardship; the Bible says He causes it. Yes—read it again: "I am the LORD, and there is no other, the One forming light and creating darkness, causing well-being and creating calamity; I am the LORD who does all these."

It's an amazing statement. We love the good news. Everybody is in favor of the God who says, "I am the One who causes well-being." But most of us struggle with the God of the Bible who goes on to say, "Wait! I'm not only the Author of well-being, I'm the One who creates calamity." Whoa. How can we marry those two facts about God?

Here's the truth: God created a world in which we have the freedom to choose right or wrong, good or bad, sin or righteousness. God is not the author of sin, but He is the One who created a world in which we can choose. And from our choices flow the sin and suffering we see all around us. Much of the pain in our world is the direct consequence of individual sin. But there is also the suffering we all must bear as members of a fallen race. The effects of a sinful humanity show up randomly in human sickness, natural disasters, and the very process of aging itself. While God does not hurl these hardships at individual people or nations, He most often refuses to prevent the

"Man proposes, but God disposes."[1]

–Thomas à Kempis

Isaiah 45:6-7
*"I am the LORD, and there is no other,
The One forming light and creating darkness,
Causing well-being and creating calamity;
I am the LORD who does all these."*

fallout from a fallen world. In that sense it can accurately be said that God is the author of a world in which calamity does strike.

In spite of that reality, the world He made is a good one for all who receive the gifts He offers freely. Into this world of sin and suffering God does not hesitate to say, "I'm the One who made the world this way, and if you trust me you will see that My ultimate plan is good."

⑥ **Your memory verse for this week is a promise of what God does for those who love Him and are called according to His purposes. Fill in the blanks to remind yourself of that promise.**

"We know that _____ causes _____ things to work

together for _____ to those who _____ God, to those

who are _____ according to His _____" (Rom. 8:28).

The next verse in Romans 8 describes God's ultimate purpose or goal for which He causes all things to work together for your good. "For those whom He foreknew, He also predestined to become conformed to the image of His Son" (Rom. 8:29). God wants you to look and act and think like Jesus. Just as a refiner's fire is required to remove the impurities from precious metals like gold or silver, God uses troubles and difficulties to shape you into the image of Christ, His Son. When you face the trials and suffering that are common to life, remember that God permits such things; but He also can use such things to make you more like Christ than you have ever been.

⑦ **Knowing you can come out of difficulty more like your Savior Jesus Christ, are you willing to face the trials God, in His perfect love and wisdom, permits to come your way?** ❑ Yes ❑ No

⑧ **If your answer is yes, use the margin to write a prayer of submission to the Lord and His refining processes. If your answer is no, write a prayer asking the Lord to help you be more open in how you handle trials He permits in your life.**

God brings eventual well-being for those who turn to Him regardless of any hardship He may allow. Eventual calamity, however, awaits those who reject Him regardless of how well their immediate life may be going. God ensures His desired ends regardless of the choices we make. His total and complete sovereignty blows the circuits of our finite minds.

As I write this, I'm praying for a married couple on our church staff. Last weekend they received news that the wife's father had suddenly died of a heart attack. They're not completely sure whether he knew the Lord, though they had shared and prayed with him many times. In the midst of this heartache, the wife was at the very

God uses troubles and difficulties to shape you into the image of Christ, His Son.

end of her pregnancy. Two days after her dad's death she went into labor and delivered a healthy baby girl. Imagine the conflict of emotions: grief weighing heavy on her heart at the death of her dad and joy as she brought her daughter into the world.

We're quick to embrace the God who calls Himself the author of life. "Yes, that's God! God's the One who brought that beautiful baby into the world." But wait. God is also the One who took that father out and said, "His days are completed." Then we begin to ask, "God, how could You allow that to happen? Why now, God? Why at the same time? And we poke our finger in the face of a sovereign God.

It isn't wrong to ask questions. Asking questions is essential to a growing faith, provided you look for and discover the wonderful answers that are available and then let the mysteries that remain be just that—mysteries hidden in the heart of sovereignty.

⑨ **If you could ask God two questions about the presence of evil and suffering in our world or about His sovereignty, what would you ask Him?**

1. _____

2. _____

🌿 **Close today's study in prayer. Take some time to thank God for the good and well-being you have received from Him. Be specific about the things and times for which you are thankful. Then thank Him for the trials He has used to make you more like Jesus. Again, be specific.**

DAY THREE *Two Questions About God's Sovereignty*

🌿 Read Today's Walk in the Word verse in the margin, meditate on God's name, and on the next page talk to the Lord in prayer as you begin today's study.

Today's Walk in the Word
Isaiah 45:5—" 'I am the Lord, and there is no other; Besides Me there is no God.' "

Meditate on God's Name
The head over all rule and authority (Colossians 2:10)

God sometimes shows us His purposes but then often does not. That raises two questions. One is theological—a thinking question; the other is very practical—a question of the heart that addresses how we feel. Let me try to answer them both.

First, the theological question: If God really controls all things, then how can He hold us responsible for the sinful choices we make?

Talk to the Lord

Sovereign God, I do believe that You alone are God. You rule the universe and everything in it. All authority belongs to You. I am comforted to know that You are in control even when I do not understand. Amen.

Review Your Memory Verse

Romans 8:28—*"We know that God causes all things to work together for good to those who love God, to those who are called according to His purpose."*

Remember that He is God and we are not.

In other words, if God is really sovereign and in control, do I have a free will? Do I choose to sin or does God determine I will sin? Am I strung up like Pinocchio, under the hands of some mega-Geppetto? Let's try to answer that, and then we can look at the heart question which naturally follows.

Question 1: Am I just a puppet?

• Moses called out to the entire nation of Israel, " 'I have set before you life and death, the blessing and the curse. So choose life' " (Deut. 30:19).
• Joshua stood above the nation of Israel, lifted his voice and called upon them, " 'Choose for yourselves today whom you will serve: … but as for me and my house, we will serve the LORD' " (Josh. 24:15).
• Jesus stood on a grassy hill in Galilee and said, "Come to Me, all who are weary and heavy-laden, and I will give you rest" (Matt. 11:28).
• Our Lord also called out to the massive crowds that heard Him preach, " 'If anyone wishes to come after Me, he must deny himself, and take up his cross and follow Me' " (Mark 8:34).

Moses and Joshua gave a choice to Israel. Jesus gave a choice to "Whosoever will … ." Was Jesus saying, "Whosoever will may come," but snickering under His breath, "that is, if I called you. Otherwise you are so up the creek"? No—that's ridiculous! Obviously, Christ was teaching that we have a choice to make.

① **Which of the following is true about your choice to follow the Lord? Check one.**
  ❑ a. God invites me to choose, but He really doesn't mean it. He's already made my choice for me.
  ❑ b. God invites me to choose, and I have the freedom to choose to follow Him or not follow Him.

You absolutely have a choice. Christ calls and we choose if we are going to respond. This is no game. It's reality.

"But wait," I hear you say. "Ephesians 1:11 says that God determines all things according to the counsel of His will." That's true, too. God is absolutely sovereign in all things. We also have a free will to make life choices for which we will give an account.

There are things God has not explained and there are tensions between some of the truths He has revealed. Those tensions are called mysteries. To live with them comfortably, just try to remember that He is God and we are not.

Deuteronomy 29:29 says that "the hidden things belong to the LORD our God, but the revealed things belong to us and our children forever" (HCSB). There are a small number of truths in the Bible that are difficult to reconcile within the limitations of our own minds. These are the secret or hidden things that belong only to God. There is far more benefit in focusing on the things which have been revealed by the Lord.

② **Based on what you have studied thus far, are you a puppet controlled by God's determinations or are you free to make choices to follow Him or not? Check one.**
   ❑ a. I have no say in my life. I'm just a puppet controlled by God.
   ❑ b. I have the freedom to choose. God invites me to choose to follow Him.

I'm not embarrassed to tell you that there is some stuff about God that I don't get. I'm more concerned when I hear people talk like they have it all figured out. Throughout church history, people who have tried to solve the tension between the sovereignty of God and the free will of humans have ended up with a pile of Scriptures they constantly repeat and a second pile they seem to ignore. Humanity's free will and God's sovereignty are two parallel lines that meet only in the mind of our Creator, a paradox we will never fully comprehend in this life. Both are true. God is sovereign and humans have a free will.

PARADOX
an apparent contradiction, an ambiguity

Two Illustrations of This Mystery

Following are two illustrations that have helped me relax about this mystery. Imagine we are taking a cruise to England. The ocean liner has left New York enroute to Liverpool. Nobody is going to stop it. You and I are playing ping-pong and other people are swimming in the pool. Passengers are doing their own thing all over the boat. Each is making choices. Yet the choices we make don't affect the fact that this ocean liner is going to England and nothing is going to stop it. In that way, God has set some sovereign purposes in this world. The little choices we make will never alter His ultimate purposes. I choose what to do on the boat, but either way it's going to England.

A few years ago I was in Indonesia and got to play against a chess master. I'm a lousy chess player, and it was brutal. There were 10 of us, each with a chessboard set up, and he played us all at the same time. He would walk down the row of boards, crushing each of us with his speed and incredibly insightful moves. In 15 minutes we were all out of the game. It was crazy!

In some ways that's a bit how God works. We make our moves, but God's purposes are not affected by them. He has always known both what we would choose and what He would do. But don't think that God is playing a game with us. God made all His moves in eternity past! We're stuck in time; God is not. He's not limited to our little life calendar. He is eternal. He completely controls the universe—with His feet up! He's not stretched or stressed in any way. That's what it means to be sovereign.

③ **Circle the word or words in the following statement that make(s) it true.**

God is sovereign, and I (am / am not) just a puppet.

But that may not be where you struggle with the issue of God's sovereignty. It may not bother you to think that God controls consequences and that God produces outcomes. Can I guess where it is you might struggle with sovereignty? Is it when painful circumstances come that are not the direct result of choices you have made? That issue gets us to our second question about sovereignty.

> God's love is not a pampering love. God's love is a perfecting love.

Question 2: How can a loving God allow so much suffering?

God's love is not a pampering love. God's love is a perfecting love. God does not get up every day trying to figure how He can plant a bigger smile on your face. God is in the process of growing us and changing us. His love is a transforming love.

Hebrews 12:6 tells us that "whom the Lord loves He disciplines, and He scourges every son whom He receives." If you are without God's discipline, the Bible says you are not really one of His children. So sometimes within the framework of sovereignty, God's love says, "I will allow this for a particular purpose." Preferring the meaningful worship of a few to the robotic worship of the masses, God chose to make a world in which people would have the freedom to follow or reject Him. In making that world God knew that some would reject Him and all of the pain in our fallen world would be the result.

Sometimes God takes hold of that "fallenness" and uses it to chasten and grow His own children. He offers His comforting, abiding presence to His children who endure the exact same kinds of things as those who know nothing of His mercy and grace. Bad things do happen to good people. God is sovereign even over that.

④ **Which of the following are reasons God permits human suffering. Check all that apply.**
   ❑ a. God wants to see how much He can torture people before they break.
   ❑ b. God disciplines and corrects His wayward children because of His perfect love.
   ❑ c. God gets glory for Himself by the manner in which His children endure suffering victoriously.
   ❑ d. God strengthens and matures His children as they endure the stresses of undeserved but unavoidable human suffering.
   ❑ e. God takes pleasure in making people miserable and watching them suffer.

Did you check b, c, and d? You're correct. Good job!

Helen Rosevere was a British medical missionary to the Congo during the uprising of revolutionaries. Though she had gone to the Congo to serve God and to share the gospel, this pure, gracious, innocent woman of God was humiliated and raped; but she hung on with her life to a faith in God that refused to be shaken. While she was recovering, Helen leaned hard on the Lord.

As you go through a painful circumstance, you either get closer to the Lord or further away. Trials will always push you. Either they wedge between you and God—pushing you out from Him or the weight of those same burdens drives you closer to Him. If today you are broken, feeling crushed by the weight of a trial, you have a choice. You can harden your heart and refuse the sovereign purposes of God that will one day prove good, or you can run to Him and participate in the blessing God has planned. Choose to bury your face and even your tears in the mystery of His sovereignty. It's a hard choice, but one you will never regret.

Recovering from her ordeal in the Congo, Helen wrote a question as though spoken from God's own mouth: Can you thank Me for trusting you with this experience even if I never tell you why?

⑤ **Can you thank God for trusting you with the hardest and most painful experiences of your life?**
❏ Yes ❏ No ❏ Not yet ❏ Only some of them

Sometimes we act as the mighty inquisitors, demanding to know: "Why did You do this?" We foolishly say, "I won't trust You if You don't show me why!" We expect that somehow God reveals the answers and conforms His behavior to our narrow intellects. What we fail to see is that we are the ones who are on trial and that our incessant questioning reveals more about us than it does about God.

The Scottish author George MacDonald said, "I find that doing the will of God leaves me no time for disputing about His plans." For some right now that's tough to hear, but God is giving you grace and time to sort these things through. With His help you can get to sovereignty even if the top of that mountain is swallowed up in mist—a mystery.

🍃 **Look at the mountain in the margin as an illustration of those times when you have faced suffering or loss and have not known why. Close today's study by voicing a prayer accepting God's sovereignty when the reasons for your experiences remain hidden in mystery.**

> "Can you thank Me for trusting you with this experience even if I never tell you why?"

DAY FOUR *God's Sovereignty at Work in You*

🍃 **Read Today's Walk in the Word verse in the margin. On the next page meditate on God's name, and talk to the Lord in prayer as you begin today's study.**

God Draws You to Himself in Salvation

Isaiah says, "Israel has been saved by the LORD with an everlasting salvation" (45:17). God is the One who saves. As one of the billions of people on this earth, if your eyes have been opened to the truth that can be found only in the gospel of Jesus Christ, if you've turned from

Today's Walk in the Word
Isaiah 45:9—" 'Woe to the one
    who quarrels with his Maker—
An earthenware vessel among
    the vessels of earth!
Will the clay say to the potter,
    "What are you doing?" ' "

Jesus Christ, ... the Ruler of the kings of the earth (Revelation 1:5)

Talk to the Lord
My Maker, You are the Potter and I am clay in Your hands. You did a good work in my life when you called me to salvation. You are working to mold me into a beautiful and useful vessel. I surrender to what You are doing in my life. Be Lord and Ruler in my life. Amen.

Review Your Memory Verse
Romans 8:28—*"We know that God causes all things to work together for good to those who love God, to those who are called according to His purpose."*

SANCTIFICATION
the process where God transforms a converted sinner into Christlikeness

your sin and embraced Christ as the only basis for your forgiveness, you are numbered among the few on the narrow road to eternal life. The fact that you are off the broad road to destruction is a sovereign act of Almighty God.

You say, "But I chose. I chose!" Yes, you did. But somehow in all of that, God was choosing too. Jesus said, "'no one can come to Me, unless the Father who sent me draws him'" (John 6:44). In His grace, God sovereignly chooses to set His love upon His people. If you are among the few who truly know Him, consider yourself among the most blessed people in history.

① **Name one way God's sovereignty has been at work in your life.**

_____

God Is Sanctifying You
Sanctification is the term that describes the process by which God takes converted sinners and transforms their character. If you're in Christ, God is sanctifying you; He is changing you. Look at Isaiah 45:8-9:

> "Drip down, O heavens, from above,
> And let the clouds pour down righteousness;
> Let the earth open up and salvation bear fruit,
> And righteousness spring up with it.
> I, the LORD, have created it.
> "Woe to the one who quarrels with his Maker."

② **Underline that last line.**

It's a pronouncement of judgment. What do you think it means to quarrel with God? Isaiah draws two pictures to answer that question.

> "An earthenware vessel among the vessels of earth!
> Will the clay say to the potter, 'What are you doing?'
> Or the thing you are making say, 'He has no hands?'
> "Woe to him who says to a father, 'What are you begetting?'
> Or to a woman, 'To what are you giving birth?'" (vv. 9-10).

We would never look at a newborn baby and shriek to his or her parents, "Who made this hideous child?" Nor would a vessel on the potter's wheel come to life and say, "Get your hands off me, I don't want a handle there!" Isaiah wanted to illustrate how ridiculous we sound when we try to direct God's hand.

③ **Name a second way God's sovereignty is at work in your life.**

_____

Remember Bill Cosby's famous line for parents and kids in conflict? "Watch out, child—I brought you into this world and I can take you out." We laugh at this parental sovereignty! God is sovereign. He breathed life into us, and He sustains it every moment. If you draw another breath in this moment, it's because He approves. All that we are belongs to the sovereign King of the universe. That's why we must try to avoid flippantly asking, "What are You doing?"

Look at the verse again. "Woe to the one who quarrels with His Maker." After 15 years of pastoral experience, I can report this as the place where most people struggle spiritually. God has allowed some hardship into your life. Maybe it's your work situation. Maybe it's a marital struggle or a prolonged health crisis. You could be facing a profound loneliness that won't go away, or a deep and sudden loss that time will never completely fill. The choice is easy to understand but terrifically difficult to make and stick with. It's this: "Either I'm going to get bent and eventually bitter, or I am going to allow God to be God."

Will you trust that God will bring a good purpose through your yieldedness to Him? Or are you going to fight and resist and spend your whole life wondering why you can't be the lady across the street? Key question: Are you going to embrace the life your sovereign God has allowed? The alternative is a life of bitterness.

④ **As you review the difficulties you have faced in your life, would you say you've embraced God's sovereignty or have you become bitter? Check your response or write your own.**
   ❑ a. I'm afraid I've developed bitterness and questioned God's goodness.
   ❑ b. I try to let God shape me and teach me through the difficulties.
   ❑ c. I've had mixed responses: some of a and some of b.
   ❑ d. Other:_____

Choosing to Live in His Victory
When many people think of Corrie ten Boom, they think of a courageous older lady who traveled the world in the 1950s to 1980s sharing with millions God's message of forgiveness. But don't think that Corrie's message of forgiveness came easily to her. Corrie's battle to accept God's sovereignty had been fought in the living hell that was the Ravensbruck concentration camp where 92,000 women died (WWII). As Corrie's sister Betsie lay dying in the camp hospital, she described God's sovereignty in a way that changed Corrie forever:

> I don't know why God allows suffering, Corrie, all I know is across the blueprint of our lives, God wrote the word Ravensbruck. ... Tell them, Corrie—tell them that no pit is so deep that He is not deeper still. They will listen to you because we have been here.[2]

None of us get to choose the words that are written across the blueprint of our lives. The only choice we have is whether we are going to submit to a sovereign God or shake our fist and demand answers not intended for this life. That's the choice we get. Corrie later said,

> Are you going to embrace the life your sovereign God has allowed? The alternative is a life of bitterness.

> "No pit is so deep that He is not deeper still."[2]

> "The higher view we have of His sovereignty—that our times are in His hands—the greater will be the possibility to live in His victory."[3]

"The higher view we have of His sovereignty—that our times are in His hands—the greater will be the possibility to live in His victory."[3] The choice you make at this point determines the person you are the rest of your life.

The same sun that melts the ice also hardens the clay. The difference between people is not the circumstances we go through, but how we chose to deal with those circumstances. That's what determines who lives on the peak and who lives in the valley. The good news is that, by God's design, you are free to make your choice.

🌿 **Close today's study by spending some time reflecting on the difficult times God has permitted in your life. Think about the ways you have chosen to respond. If you've argued with your Maker, ask Him to forgive you. For the times He has worked through difficulties to grow you and sanctify you, thank Him. Consider writing a journal entry listing some of the ways God has been working in your life through His sovereignty.**

DAY FIVE *Responding to God's Sovereignty*

Today's Walk in the Word
Isaiah 66:2—
" 'To this one I will look,
To him who is humble and
*   contrite of spirit, and who*
*   trembles at My word.' "*

Meditate on God's Name
Our only Master and Lord,
Jesus Christ (Jude 4)

Talk to the Lord
Master and Lord, Jesus Christ, I love You because You first loved me and gave Your life on a cross to purchase my forgiveness. I'm Yours now. You bought me and paid for me. I choose to follow You as my Master and Lord. Speak and I'll obey. Amen.

🌿 **Read Today's Walk in the Word verse in the margin, meditate on God's name, and talk to the Lord in prayer as you begin today's study.**

God's sovereignty is not just some concept to admire. It is a reality to embrace. Let's explore three ways you can choose to embrace God's sovereignty.

Principle 1: I will be obedient when told.
In your heart determine that "when God's Word says something, I will obey it. When God's Word says 'go here,' I'm going. When God's Word says 'wait' or 'trust,' that's what I'll do. When God's Word says 'live in this righteous way,' I'm going after that with my whole heart."

① **Write the first principle IF you are ready to choose obedience.**

_____

For God to guide you through His Word, you need to be reading and studying it regularly. As you read, ask the Holy Spirit to guide your understanding. Then ask, "What do I need to do to obey?"

② Take a moment to reflect. Has God already revealed something you were to obey and you know you have not yet obeyed? If so, make a note and choose now to obey Him.

_____

_____

Write Your Memory Verse
Romans 8:28

_____

_____

_____

_____

Principle 2: I will be righteous when tempted.

We all have temptation points when we feel pulled toward sin. You know what you struggle with, as I know where I'm weakest. The next time you're tempted, remember Isaiah 45:8: "Drip down, O heavens, from above, and let the clouds pour down righteousness; let the earth open up and salvation bear fruit, and righteousness spring up with it. I, the Lord, have created it." God uses the earth metaphorically to picture the righteousness that springs up in our lives when we have victory over temptation. It's a virtual garden of righteousness!

God says in Isaiah 66:2, "To this one I will look, to him who is humble and contrite of spirit, and who trembles at My word." God is promising that He totally takes care of those who embrace His plan and His Word. Remember, willing obedience reveals a heart that is embracing sovereignty. And God says in Isaiah 45:8 that it's His responsibility to fill your life with righteousness. The choosing is yours, but the righteousness itself comes from Him. Consecrate yourself afresh to be the man or woman God has created you to be. Commit to choosing righteousness when you are tempted.

③ **Write the second principle IF you are ready to choose righteousness.**

_____

④ **Think about one area where you seem to face temptation most frequently. Decide now how you will respond when you are tempted.**

Principle 3: I will be submissive when tried.

This is perhaps the most difficult of the three principles. In the midst of the trial say, "I'm going to submit to God even though I don't know why He has allowed this, and I don't know what He is doing. I am going to humble myself before God and believe He has a purpose I will someday understand. I reject bitterness and hard-heartedness, and I choose to become submissive and wait."

When you willingly take from God's hand whatever He allows, believing that eternity will prove His wisdom and goodness even though you can't see it now, you are embracing sovereignty at the deepest level. And you are preparing your life for a joy so immense that few ever truly experience it.

> Willing obedience reveals a heart that is embracing sovereignty.

> "I'm going to submit to God. … I reject bitterness and hard-heartedness, and I choose to become submissive and wait."

⑤ **Write the third principle IF you are ready to choose submission. Then write in the margin a pledge of your submission to the Lord, knowing that your loving Heavenly Father has a desire for you to experience His best.**

God's Sovereignty Celebrated

Because God is sovereign, He is able to do exactly as He pleases. What He pleases for you is to know Him through all the experiences of your life now and someday, in the fullness of joy that only eternity can reveal. If that truth does not comfort you, it is because you are still fighting a war you can never win. God is sovereign; and there is incredible comfort in embracing what He chooses to allow, especially when that is most difficult for you. Someday we will stand with saints from every age of history and worship God for who He is—the righteous Ruler and the sovereign LORD. In that day we will overflow with joy at the infinite wisdom and immeasurable splendor of all God has chosen and performed. "From Him and through Him and to Him are all things" (Rom. 11:36).

When you embrace that fully in the deepest part of who you are, only then do you know what it means to be gripped by the sovereignty of God. Make the choice now to bow in submission before your Sovereign. As you do that genuinely from your heart, you will be gripped by truly knowing (in a way that seeing could never accomplish) that God's sovereign purposes will prove loving and good.

Do you tremble at God's Word? Are you worried that obedience to Scripture will be overwhelming? Too costly? What God-directed change are you resisting right now? Are you willing to change? If your honest answer to this final question is no, then ask God to make you willing to follow His way. You'll be amazed that someday soon your heart will begin to say, "You have the right to reign over me. I will go where you tell me, do what you ask. Because you are in control."

My Declarations

- I'm done resisting God.
- I'm not going to fight Him anymore.
- I'm not going to run from Him.
- I'm not going to turn to my own way of thinking, rationalizing, or manipulating the circumstances.
- I am going to embrace this situation as from the hand of a sovereign and loving God.
- I am going to trust that He knows what He is doing … in my life, in the lives of those I love, and in the world.

⑥ **On a piece of paper, copy "My Declarations" from the margin, date it, sign it, and keep it in your Bible for regular review and renewal.**

Being gripped by God's sovereignty doesn't take away your questions, but it will take away your anxiety. Determine today to surrender your "why?" questions to God. From your will, release God to resolve or not resolve any issue that looms large in your life. Ask God to make this a turning point in your lifelong walk with Him. Live with the mystery of how He is working all things together for your good even when you cannot see it or even imagine how. (See Romans 8:28 and Ephesians 1:11-12.)

Being gripped by God's sovereignty also declares war on human pride. When you ask God to reveal His greatness, you will be overwhelmed with the miniature you compared to infinity itself. Respond with humility and glad surrender to the righteous Ruler of the universe.

⑦ Expression is an important part of the learning process. Share with a friend or family member what you are learning about God's sovereignty and His greatness in this study. Your expression will encourage you both. Review this week's study for key points. Write a few notes of what you will share in the margin

Time to Give it Up!

Maybe you find as I do that when your heart is gripped afresh by God's sovereignty, there's nothing left to do but resign your life to Him. You hear His call to "lay it all down," and experience the joy of total unqualified surrender.

If you make that decision, if you follow through and really begin to live the life that is totally and completely submitted to God's awesome purposes, you will never regret it—not for a moment. I promise!

🍃 **Close this week's study with the following prayer. Pray it slowly and thoughtfully. Personalize it. Make it your own.**

Sovereign LORD, I thank You by faith for something I don't completely understand. Thank You for being in control of all. Others who have gone through valleys like I am facing have testified to Your faithfulness. I ask for your grace as I choose by faith to take my eyes off my experience and wait in hope to see your sovereign purposes revealed. Whether in this life or in the life to come, I am believing that you are good and do all things well.

At times I don't see it and even now I don't feel it, but I will not let those things rule my faith. You are good. Generations have tasted and seen that You are good. I believe Your Word and by faith I submit to your sovereignty.

Father, You are good. Lord, You are faithful. I trust You. I submit to You. I worship You. In the name of Jesus I pray. Amen.

---

[1] Thomas à Kempis, *The Imitation of Christ, Bartlett's Quotations* [online, cited 29 August 2005]. Available from the Internet: *www.bartleby.com/100/112.1.html.*

[2] *The Hiding Place,* World Wide Pictures: A Billy Graham Evangelistic Association Ministry, 1975.

[3] Corrie ten Boom, in Pamela Rosewell Moore "Things I Learned from Corrie."

GRIPPED BY THE GREATNESS OF GOD

GRIPPED BY THE WORKS OF GOD

Follow the session plans in the leader's guide on page 141.

Discussion Guide on God's Sovereignty

1. What have you learned or experienced about God's sovereignty this week that has been most meaningful or life changing?
2. How would you summarize the meaning of God's sovereignty? (activity 3, p. 58)
3. If you could ask God two questions about the presence of evil and suffering in our world or about His sovereignty, what would you want to ask Him and why? (activity 9, p. 65)
4. In a discussion of God's sovereignty, Suppose a person were to ask your class: "If God is all-powerful and He is in control of the universe, am I just a puppet?" How would you answer him?
5. Suppose someone asked, "How can a loving God allow so much human suffering?" How would you answer her? What are some reasons God permits human suffering? Does He ever cause suffering? (see activity 4, p. 68)
6. Review the three principles on pages 72-73. As you apply these principles in your life, what difference will they make?

DVD Message Notes on God's Works (21 minutes)

1. In God we find amazing _____.
   - He's always available—just what we need to quench our thirst.
   - He is free, but you have to give _____.
   - Satisfaction can only be found in _____.
   - The soul of man needs God.

2. In God we find abundant _____.
  • Misunderstandings of God's reception: _____ God, anxious God, ambivalent God
  • You have to _____ your wicked ways (Isa. 55:7).
  • God chooses not to remember our _____ (Ps. 103:12; Mic. 7:19).
  • What we think about _____: Who? How much? How often?
  • God's forgiveness: His _____ and ways are beyond our understanding.

Responding to the Message

In small groups discuss your response to the following:
1. What characteristic or experience of God has brought you the greatest satisfaction in your life and why?
2. How did you come to God to experience His abundant pardon? Do you have an experience of sovereignty dropping a boulder on your life? If so, what was the name on your boulder? Share your story.

Preview Statements for This Week's Study

• In God we find amazing satisfaction.
• In God we find abundant pardon.
• In God's Word we find accomplished truth.
• In God's works we find absolute delight.
• There is in every human heart a tendency "to leave the God we love" unless we are continually gripped by His greatness.
• Experiencing the greatness of God is like a satisfying meal to the starving and like a drink of cold water to a man in the desert.
• Leave what anchors your heart to the emptiness of this world, and return to God as your passion and priority.
• When we return to the Lord, He welcomes us back in love.

Snapshot Summary
Stop and look, observe the incredible work that God is doing in this world. Find your highest joy and deepest satisfaction by entering into that work.

My Goal for You
I want you to understand God's abundant pardon and the work of His Word in such a way that you know joy and satisfaction in Him.

Key Verse to Memorize
Isaiah 55:11—"'So will My word be which goes forth from My mouth;
It will not return to Me empty,
Without accomplishing what I desire,
And without succeeding in the matter for which I sent it.'"

(Message Notes blanks: satisfaction, yourself, God, pardon, angry, forsake, sins, forgiveness, thoughts)

This Week's Mountaintop in Isaiah—Isaiah 55 (Selected Verses)

[1] "Every one who thirsts, come to the waters; and you who have no money come, buy and eat. Come, buy wine and milk without money and without cost.
[3] "Incline your ear and come to Me. Listen, that you may live; and I will make an everlasting covenant with you, according to the faithful mercies shown to David.

[5] "Behold, you will call a nation you do not know, and a nation which knows you not will run to you, because of the LORD your God, even the Holy One of Israel; for he has glorified you."
[6] Seek the LORD while He may be found; call upon Him while He is near.
[7] Let the wicked forsake his way and the unrighteous man his

thoughts; and let him return to the LORD, and He will have compassion on him, and to our God, for He will abundantly pardon.
[8] "For My thoughts are not your thoughts, neither are your ways My ways," declares the LORD.
[9] "As the heavens are higher than the earth, so are my ways higher than your ways and my thoughts than your thoughts."

It Happened to Me

① **I want to tell you about a faithful saint who was gripped by God's works. As you read Roy's story, underline characteristics, attitudes, or behaviors that are worth imitating. I've underlined one for you.**

Roy and his wife Carol were among the 18 people whom God first gave a vision for the church that became Harvest Bible Chapel. I remember when Roy talked with me about pastoring this soon-to-be church. He had a passion for the things of God like few men his age (he was 61).

When Harvest celebrated 16 years of ministry, you could still find <u>Roy serving and singing</u>, still fired up about God's Word. His hair had thinned a bit, his health had faltered, but there was a flash in his eyes as he talked about what he currently saw God doing. God still drew Roy's heart like a magnet. And on any given Sunday, people would line up to pray with him after every service. Why? Because it was obvious Roy was gripped by God's greatness.

Roy exemplified a person who loved and laughed and reveled in God's wonderful work his whole life. It kept him in the race and on course. Roy is one reason I love to be around faithful men and women who have followed after the greatness of God for half a century or more. By watching their lives, you see what can be. Once you've seen it, nothing less can satisfy.

Not long ago the phone rang at home, and it was our associate senior pastor. I could tell by his voice that something was wrong, and as he took a deep breath, I found myself doing the same.

"James, I am over at Roy's, and just a few moments ago he went to be with the Lord."

Time stood still in that moment as my mind flooded with a thousand memories. In a split-second, Roy was gone from this life and entered the next.

Normally at such a critical moment I would have leapt from my chair and rushed to the side of the grieving. But this was different, I was the one grieving the loss of a dear friend and fellow leader. I needed some time to gather myself before the Lord, or I would not have anything to give to others. I sat in that chair for over an hour, reviewing the record of Roy's life, so well-lived, so deeply steeped in the experience and observation of God's work.

Roy was truly a founder in our church. When we lost some founding members to division and needless separation, Roy was the strength that brought us to Christ and held us all together. Roy was the thermostat for this young pastor prone to overheating. He had the ability to calm my troubled soul and get me back on task, showing me how to trust God, how to wait on God, and always, always showing me grace and forgiveness.

He was number one at welcoming others and the force that found and fed our few seniors. Roy was quick to laugh and slow to judge. He was easily grieved by harshness or haughtiness. Roy was the visionary who found our first church property and followed my leadership even when the future was uncertain. He was a man who was gripped by the works of God.

Not surprisingly, his wake was standing room only. Fifty yards of mourners lined the church lobby for hours waiting for a chance to repeat the refrain: "God worked in my life through Roy when … ." The hours raced by and the stories never got old. The funeral was a celebration. Children and grandchildren stood through their tears and rehearsed their own experience of God at work through Roy.

I'm telling you, there is no life better than this. Roy had been taken and shaken by God many years ago, and God never released his grip.

Do you have that? Have you been gripped by the works of God? Have you experienced His satisfaction? His abundant pardon? The power of His Word penetrating your heart? Do you want to experience that again? Even now?

Roy had this going on big-time and you can too, but you must express yourself. I know this for a fact because I saw it in Roy and … because it happened to me!

DAY ONE *Get a Grip on God's Works*

🍃 Read Today's Walk in the Word verse in the margin, meditate on God's name, and talk to the Lord in prayer as you begin today's study.

① Isaiah 55:11 (Today's Walk in the Word) is a powerful description of the work God accomplishes through His Word. I want you to memorize it. Start now and fill in the blanks.

"'So will My _____ be which goes forth from My _____;

It will not _____ to Me _____, without

_____ what I _____, and without

_____ in the _____ for which I _____ it.'"

One of the darkest places in my Christian experience is the grief I feel over Christians who quit—especially leaders I know who used to be in the race and stretching for the tape with their whole hearts. What happened, and why did they pack it in?

I've heard it said that the crises of life reveal something that has been happening for a long time. We tend to focus on the shock of the tire blowing out, but in reality there were a lot of maintenance issues that preceded the flashing lights and the flares by the side of the highway. Somewhere, much earlier on, they lost their longing for God.

The fear of following in their footsteps sometimes haunts me. Do you know what I mean? I sure don't want to crawl across the finish line a defeated, derailed Christian or worse—give up the race before the final stretch even starts. No, I would guess that like me you want to break that tape with arms high and your face toward the sun and say with the apostle Paul, "I have finished the course, I have kept the faith" (2 Tim. 4:7).

② **Think about Christian saints you have known. Name one who is finishing or has finished his or her spiritual race in a style worthy of our Savior. Then name one (first name or initials) who seems to be withdrawn from active duty and far from fellowship with God.**

_____   _____

In every human heart there is a tendency "to leave the God we love" unless we are continually gripped by His greatness, unless we allow

---

Today's Walk in the Word
Isaiah 55:11—"'So will My word be which goes forth from My mouth;
It will not return to Me empty,
Without accomplishing what I desire,
And without succeeding in the matter for which I sent it.'"

Meditate on God's Name
The Author and Perfecter of faith (Hebrews 12:2)

Talk to the Lord
Father God, Your works are mighty and marvelous. What You determine to do happens. What You begin, You finish. Thank You for being the Author and Perfecter of my faith. Reveal to me this week the works You have available for me to experience. Amen.

2 Timothy 4:7—*"I have finished the course, I have kept the faith."*

our hearts and minds to be rocked with the truth of all that He is on a regular basis.

AWOL
Away Without Leave, a military term for people who have left their place of service without permission

③ **If you had to rate your life on a continuum from AWOL (1) to Finishing in Spiritual Style (10), where would you rate yourself spiritually? Place an X on the line below.**

1	2	3	4	5	6	7	8	9	10
AWOL								Finishing in Spiritual Style	

WHY WALK WITH GOD?

A life experiencing God's best—that's the kind of life Isaiah spreads out in front of us in chapter 55. In beautiful detail, he describes the benefits of walking with God over the long haul. They are:

- Permanent and complete satisfaction with the things of God
- Abundance this world knows nothing about
- Immeasurable forgiveness—that transforms your heart and transfers to others
- Truth that takes root in your life and produces a bumper crop of "God-confidence" year after year

④ **In the items above, underline these four words and then check the one that interests you most in this week's study.**
❏ Satisfaction ❏ Forgiveness
❏ Abundance ❏ "God-confidence"

These are the works of God that keep people's hearts beating after Him for 50, 60, or 70 years. And it's all in Isaiah 55. Nowhere else in the Bible do we read a chapter packed more fully with God's invitation to personally experience His works. Only here can we read such conviction about God's great deeds designed before the foundation of the world. Nothing can stop Him. You might as well try to keep the rain from falling.

AN INVITATION TO EXPERIENCE GOD'S WORKS

Is that the kind of refreshment you need for your marathon in God? C'mon, run alongside me for a while; I want to show you the phenomenal work God is doing—not just a long time ago, but in our world today and potentially in our hearts during this week. It's time to be gripped by the works of God. So let's jump in!

🍃 **Close today's study by reviewing the things you underlined in Roy's story in "It Happened to Me" on page 78. Ask God to grip you with His works in your life in such a way that it is obvious to those around you.**

DAY TWO *Amazing Satisfaction and Covenant Love*

🍃 Read Today's Walk in the Word verse in the margin, meditate on God's name, and talk to the Lord in prayer as you begin today's study.

IN GOD WE FIND AMAZING SATISFACTION

I know something about you. You're thirsty for God. He has built within each of us a need that only He can satisfy. Isaiah longs for God's people to "get it"—to understand everything His promise of satisfaction can mean to them.

God wants to be for your soul what water is for your body. If you've ever been dehydrated from heavy work in the hot sun, you know that milk, sodas, and lemonade just don't cut it. When you're really thirsty, nothing satisfies like water.

① **Complete the comparison below by filling in the blank.**

Just as water satisfies a thirsty body,

_____ satisfies a thirsty soul.

We take water for granted, but in Isaiah's day you couldn't just turn on the tap for a drink. Fresh, pure, clean water was an incredible resource. Like a water-boy after football practice in the hot Texas sun, Isaiah shouts "Come and get it!" God is the satisfaction needed by a thirsty soul. So why doesn't everyone drink?

Objection #1: I can't afford it.
"That sounds really good, but I can't afford that water." Doesn't matter, Isaiah says come anyway. "You who have no money come, buy and eat" (v. 1). Hear me on this one: Nothing God wants to give you will ever cost you a dime. You think you can't afford God's gift? You're right. Everything God gives is "on Him." Everything! The next time somebody tells you that you have to do something to deserve what God offers you, call it for what it is—a lie! Everything God wants to give you is free.

Think about it. What's the biggest insult you can give someone who gives you a gift? Suppose your mom buys you a Christmas present. She's so excited to put this beautifully wrapped present in your hands and you get out your wallet and insist on reimbursing her. What an insult! Same thing for God. Eternity isn't long enough to pay for what God has done for us. That's why it comes as a gift—free!

Today's Walk in the Word
John 7:38—" 'He who believes in Me, as the Scripture said, "From his innermost being will flow rivers of living water." ' "

Meditate on God's Name
One who wipes out your transgressions (Isaiah 43:25)

Talk to the Lord
Lord Jesus, You promise to satisfy me with rivers of living water. Quench all my spiritual thirst. You are the One who forgives my sin. Remind me today of the satisfaction I can know in You and enable me to rejoice in Your amazing pardon. Amen.

Review Your Memory Verse
Isaiah 55:11—" 'So will My word be which goes forth from My mouth;
It will not return to Me empty,
Without accomplishing what I desire,
And without succeeding in the matter for which I sent it.' "

God wants to be for your soul what water is for your body.

Objection #2: I need more than water.

"Sure, water is great and everything, but I need more than water."

What?!

"No, really I do. The Bible and church—that's all great stuff. But I need more than that." Have you ever said in your heart or by your actions that God was not enough to satisfy you?

Isaiah encourages us: "You who have no money come, buy and eat. Come, buy wine and milk without money and without cost."

Not only will God satisfy our thirst with water, but He has prepared the greatest banquet ever served to feed our hungry souls. Notice who's invited—the thirsty and the penniless, those who totally admit their need for God. Do you admit your need? If so, you are invited, too. God wants to be your satisfaction.

② **If you were to object to God's offer of satisfaction, which of these two would more likely be your objection? Or have you moved beyond objections to seeing Him? Check one.**

❑ a. Objection #1: I'm afraid His satisfaction is too costly. He'll ask too much.

❑ b. Objection #2: I need much more than God to be satisfied. I could make you a list of the extras I want.

❑ c. I'm hungry and thirsty after God. Living water, wine, and milk—I'm ready to "buy and eat."

🌿 **Now's as good a time as any to begin telling God what's in your heart. If you checked *c* above, tell Him. Ask Him to fill you with all you need of Him. If you are still lingering at *a* or *b* above, don't hesitate to tell God about that, too. Ask Him to create a hunger and thirst in your heart for Him that is so intense you will settle for nothing less than Him.**

A LESSON IN SATISFACTION

Trade magazines herald him as one of rock and roll's great successes. His band, The Rolling Stones, recorded the song selected by 700 people in the music industry as the #1 rock and roll song of all time. Yet the emptiness of Mick Jagger's life calls out pathetically like that hit song, "(I Can't Get No) Satisfaction." Mick Jagger said in one interview, "I would rather be dead than singing 'Satisfaction' at [age] 45."

In 2005, he turns 62 and continues the sad refrain. It's not like he hasn't searched for satisfaction, but like so many, he is ever searching and "never able to come to the knowledge of the truth" (2 Tim. 3:7). God promises water to quench people's eternal thirst, yet they have chosen a path that leaves them eating sand.

If God is not enough, everything else in the world will never be enough. The only way you can know satisfaction in life is in a deep and fulfilling relationship with God. If you have been living apart from Him

God promises water to quench people's eternal thirst, yet they have chosen a path that leaves them eating sand.

and trying to fill that emptiness in your life with other things, please—stop! Come to Him and discover the satisfaction God alone can bring.

Experiencing the greatness of God is like a satisfying meal to the starving and a drink of cold water to a man in the desert. The psalmist agreed when he wrote: "Give thanks to the LORD , for He is good, … for He has satisfied the thirsty soul, and the hungry soul He has filled with what is good" (Ps. 107:1,9). Once you experience the real thing, you'll never long for anything else. Are you in?

③ **Where are you in this matter of satisfaction? Check one or write your own.**
　❑ a. I give thanks to the Lord. He has satisfied my thirsty soul!
　❑ b. "I can't get no satisfaction."
　❑ c. I keep seeking satisfaction, but it's like eating sand.
　❑ d. I've tasted that the Lord is good, but I'm starving for more.
　❑ e. Other:_____

GOD'S COVENANT LOVE

"I will make an everlasting covenant with you" (v. 3). A covenant is not a contract. A contract involves two people who agree to perform in a certain way. "I'll do this … you do that." If either party reneges on their part, the contract is broken.

When the Bible reveals God as a covenant God, this means God has entered into a relationship that cannot be changed by our behavior. If God were a contract God, when we acted incorrectly or lived sinfully, the contract would be broken. But a covenant is a relationship that is not dependent on the performance of one of the parties. All the responsibility lies on one side. God says, "I'm making a covenant commitment to you. I'm entering into a relationship with you that you can't mess up in any way." Sounds really permanent, doesn't it?

④ **Match the word on the left with the correct description.**
　_____ 1. Contract　　a. A relationship established by God that is dependent on His faithfulness.
　_____ 2. Covenant　　b. An agreement between two people that can be broken by one or both parties.
　　　　　　　　　　　　c. All the responsibility for the agreement lies on one side.

GOD'S LOVINGKINDNESS, MERCY, AND GRACE

(The answers to the activity 4 are 1-b, 2-a,c.) God is the ultimate promise-keeper. His name *Jehovah* reminds us that He is totally committed to humankind. He's a covenant keeping God. A covenant is very official and clearly understood by all. God's works in Isaiah 55 all find their root in His character trait, *hesed*—a Hebrew word meaning God's covenant love, His mercy and steadfast lovingkindness. Because of His *hesed*, He satisfies us with His kindness. He

Experiencing the greatness of God is like a satisfying meal to the starving and a drink of cold water to a man in the desert.

HESED
a Hebrew word meaning God's covenant love, His mercy and steadfast lovingkindness

Lamentations 3:22-23—

"For His compassions never fail. They are new every morning."

forgives us in His mercy. His life in us brings absolute delight. God's *hesed* (which Lam. 3:22-23 promises is new every morning) is the Old Testament equivalent of grace. Being gripped by God's works is to be gripped by *hesed*, God's covenantal love.

How Big Is That?

You may wonder what that relationship with God will look like. Isaiah tells us. "It's going to be like God's relationship with David." That's the illustration God chose to describe the relationship He wants to have with us: "I will make an everlasting covenant with you, according to the faithful mercies shown to David" (v. 3). David's whole life was a picture of God's mercy.

- A lion tried to kill him and God spared him (1 Sam. 17:34-37).
- A bear tried to kill him; God saved him again (1 Sam. 17:34-37).
- Then there was that whole giant thing with Goliath (1 Sam. 17).
- King Saul tried to kill David—chased him all over the country. Again and again, God protected David (1 Sam. 24).
- God put David on the throne of Israel and everything was great until the Bathsheba scandal. Even adultery and murder couldn't stop God's mercy from flowing into David's life (Ps. 32; 51).

⑤ **How would you describe the amount of God's mercy toward David? Check the one closest to your own description.**
❑ a. Huge mercy, unbelievably big
❑ b. Ordinary mercy, sounds pretty normal to me
❑ c. What mercy? Is that all?

You may at times wish God would be as generous with you. Fact is, He will be, because He promises to measure His kindness—"according to the faithful mercies shown to David."

But It's Even Bigger than That!

God says through Isaiah: "Behold, you will call a nation you do not know, and a nation which knows you not will run to you, because of the LORD your God, even the Holy One of Israel; for He has glorified you" (v. 5).

My salvation, God says, is not just about one nation anymore. What began as a specific plan for one specific people, God is spreading across the globe. God is drawing people to Himself in every country on the face of the earth. He is great—nothing can hold Him back! God says, "This thing is going to get really big. I'm going to be pardoning people all over the place." How cool is that?

🖋 **Close today's study by thanking the Lord for His love and mercy. Thank Him for entering into a covenant with you. Express your hunger and thirst for His amazing satisfaction.**

> You may at times wish God would be as generous with you. Fact is, He will!

DAY THREE · *Responding to God's Abundant Pardon*

🌿 **Read Today's Walk in the Word verse in the margin, meditate on God's name, and talk to the Lord in prayer as you begin today's study.**

God is taking people who will seek Him and call upon Him. But notice the urgency of the matter. Isaiah says, "Seek the LORD while He may be found; call upon Him while He is near" (v. 6). That implies that the hour of conviction must be the hour of decision. Scripture says, "now is 'THE DAY OF SALVATION' " (2 Cor. 6:2).

① **When is the best time to seek the Lord? Fill in the blanks.**

"while He may be _____ … while He is _____"

Is God pricking your heart about His greatness today? Whether you need to return to Him or call upon Him for the very first time by faith, you need to make that decision RIGHT NOW. Not next Friday; not a month from today; the hour of conviction has to be the hour of decision. Why? Because Genesis 6:3 says that the Spirit of God will not always strive with men. You don't know if you're going to be alive next Friday. You don't know if you're going to be in your right mind next Friday or if the Spirit of God is going to be working and stirring your heart next Friday. You don't know if you have time. If God is dealing with your heart right now, that's good news. You need to respond right now! Respond to Him today and experience the pardon.

② **Where do you stand in your need for God's abundant pardon? Check a response or write your own.**
❑ a. I've received it abundantly! Praise God.
❑ b. I've experienced the salvation side of His pardon, but I've grown lax in my holy living. I need a fresh measure of pardon.
❑ c. I've never known this kind of covenant love relationship with God. I need His pardon for all my sin.
❑ d. Other:_____

Do you need to experience His pardon? Do you say, "I want to, but how?" Look at verse 7: "Let the wicked forsake his way." If you're still offended about being called wicked, then you have some work to do. Those of us who have found the Lord understand that we have all failed Him. We say, in effect, "My life was so wrong and so lame! It was going nowhere, but I have turned from that sin and now I'm living for Him with my whole heart!" That's how you get to the Lord.

You have to forsake (leave, be done with, turn away from) those wicked ways, and, then notice the next phrase, "and the unrighteous

---

Today's Walk in the Word
Isaiah 55:7—*Let the wicked forsake his way
And the unrighteous man his thoughts;
And let him return to the LORD,
And He will have compassion on him,
And to our God,
For He will abundantly pardon.*

Meditate on God's Name
Him who loves us and released us from our sins (Revelation 1:5)

Talk to the Lord
Abundant pardon. Lord, that's surely what I need. Compassion? I need that, too. I long for a depth in my relationship with You where I experience the freedom from sin that I can know in Christ. I thank You for sending Jesus to release me from my sins. I thank You in His matchless name—Jesus. Amen.

Review Your Memory Verse
Isaiah 55:11—*" 'So will My word be which goes forth from My mouth;
It will not return to Me empty,
Without accomplishing what I desire,
And without succeeding in the matter for which I sent it.' "*

FORSAKE
leave, be done with, turn away from

man his thoughts." That's where it all begins, isn't it? In our thoughts. Wrong thinking leads to wrong living. (More on this in week 7.)

"And let him return to the LORD." *Forsake* and *return.* Those are Old Testament terms for repentance and faith. "Return to the LORD." Why? Because we can't earn our own forgiveness; it is only by faith in what the Lord has done for us that our sins can be forgiven.

Maybe you've known the Lord for many years, but your heart is not close to Him. It works the same way—forsake and return. Leave what anchors your heart to the emptiness of this world, and return to God as your passion and priority. What's holding you back? What keeps you from returning to the Lord?

I think a big issue many face is "What kind of reception am I going to get?" That was on the mind of the prodigal son in Luke 15, who lived like a fool, far from home and father. One day he woke up and said, "Am I crazy? What am I doing over here eating slop and living like a pig? I'm going to return to my father. I'm going home."

Although the son had walked away from his father, his father never stopped looking for him. When the son came to his senses, he did the "self-talk" thing all the way home. How will Dad receive me? How can I make up for what I've done? What kind of reception am I going to get? He was worried.

> Leave what anchors your heart to the emptiness of this world, and return to God as your passion and priority.

③ **Have you worried like that? What kind of reception do you think you would get if you were to return to the Lord today? Check a response or write your own.**
   ❑ a. He will be pretty angry with me for the way I've lived. He may "let me have it."
   ❑ b. He's been worried and anxious about my spiritual condition. He will be relieved when I finally come home.
   ❑ c. He won't be too concerned. After all I'm just one person. He's not all that interested in me.
   ❑ d. He's a loving Father waiting to welcome me when I come home.
   ❑ e. Other:_____

Perhaps you can relate. You ask, "What kind of response am I going to get if I return to the Lord?" I've watched people picture God in one of three ways:

FAULTY VIEWS OF GOD'S RESPONSES

1. Some people picture God as an angry God.
They think to themselves, *When I return to the Lord, He's going to stand there and say, "Do you think you can live the way you've been living and just come waltzing back in here and everything will be all fine and dandy? Well, you're wrong!"* No! God is not going to think or feel that way toward you. Maybe your dad or mom was like that, but God isn't. When we return to the Lord, He welcomes us back in love. I'll show you His actual response later.

> When we return to the Lord, He welcomes us back in love.

2. Some people picture God as an anxious God.

"Where have you been? I've been worried sick about you. I was wondering if you were ever going to come back. You've had Me up half the night!" How foolish—as if God was ever worried about anything!

3. Some people picture God as an ambivalent God.

You come into the room and He barely looks up from the newspaper. "Oh, you're back. Fine. Throw your things in the corner, and don't bother me, I'm busy." Again, that is so not God's heart.

In his wildest imagination, the runaway son in Jesus' story of the prodigal son never would have dreamt what his father did next. When the father saw him coming down the road, he got up and ran toward him. It's the only time in all Scripture that God is pictured as running. The father didn't just wait for him—he ran to him according to Luke 15:20, and threw his arms around him and fell on his neck and kissed him. He restored the son to his place as a son.

Do you see why God put that in His Word? When we are convicted of our sin and we sense our need to return to the Lord, we won't ever have to wonder, "What kind of reception am I going to get?" He showed us how He will respond.

④ **Based upon Jesus' story of the prodigal son (in the margin), how will God receive a child that comes home?**

_____

⑤ **As you read the following paragraph, underline the words that describe what God will do when we turn back to Him.**

Long ago Isaiah recorded what you can expect to get from God today. When you turn back to Him, you'll see Him running toward you. He longs to embrace you, Isaiah writes: "And He will have compassion on him, and to our God, for He will abundantly pardon" (v. 7). What a phenomenal promise.

One of my privileges as a pastor is to hear real-life stories of modern prodigals. I'm still fired up from a recent weekend when we got to hear repeated accounts of God's work in people's lives. We heard 254 life stories in all, as 254 joyous, awe-struck people were baptized. It was a great weekend of victory.

Here's what's interesting—they all told the same story. Now, if you were there you might say, "No, their stories were different." Yes, but in a deeper way they were much the same. Nearly every life had the same theme; "I was going along, thinking I was too sexy for my shirt ... and then God dropped a boulder on my life." By *boulder* I mean some crushing personal experience that obliterates pride and independence from God. The only thing different in their real-life accounts was the specific label on the boulder. For some it was a marriage crisis; others experienced a health or financial burden that caused great anxiety. Still others reported a penetrating loneliness or a profound loss that they just couldn't shake.

The Prodigal Son

"'So he got up and came to his father. But while he was still a long way off, his father saw him and felt compassion for him, and ran and embraced him and kissed him. And the son said to him, "Father, I have sinned against heaven and in your sight; I am no longer worthy to be called your son." But the father said to his slaves, "Quickly bring out the best robe and put it on him, and put a ring on his hand and sandals on his feet; and bring the fattened calf, kill it, and let us eat and celebrate; for this son of mine was dead and has come to life again; he was lost and has been found." And they began to celebrate'" (Luke 15:20-24).

"BOULDER"

some crushing personal experience that obliterates pride and independence from God

Then came God! They went on to report with different words but total unanimity that when they did turn to Him, God wasn't just a bunch of information. They experienced His forgiveness in a profound and life-altering way. That's a picture of abundant pardon.

⑥ **If you can identify with this experience of coming to Christ because a "boulder" dropped on you, write a name for that boulder below. I've listed some common ones in the margin.**

Common "Boulders"
- marriage or family crisis
- financial crisis
- job crisis or loss
- health problem
- loneliness
- depression
- purposelessness
- fear
- death of a friend or loved one
- near death experience that got your attention
- accident
- broken relationship

_____

A NEW LOOK AT FORGIVENESS

God says, "My thoughts are not your thoughts, nor are your ways My ways … For as the heavens are higher that the earth, so are My ways higher than your ways and My thoughts than your thoughts" (vv. 8-9).

I've always believed this passage taught that God is not like us; God is bigger than us. Even though that's true, that's not the primary point. Look at the context. In what ways are God's thoughts bigger than our thoughts? When He forgives; when He pardons. So, how different are our thoughts than God's thoughts about forgiveness? They're polar opposites.

⑦ **Think about your greatest concept of forgiveness or the most abundant pardon you could imagine. Imagine, for example, a sin that would involve the greatest sin against the most wonderful person or people perpetrated by the lowest and most vile sinner. What comes to your mind?**

_____

_____

Think of Saddam Hussein or Adolf Hitler and the countless innocents they have tortured and murdered. Think of the forgiveness it would take to erase all they have done. Now go deeper still, to something even worse, even harder to forgive, even more unimaginable.

Without even knowing your thoughts, I'll tell you the result—your greatest concept of forgiveness is pretty weak compared to God's thoughts. We're not even close. God says, "For as the heavens are higher that the earth" (v. 9). That's a huge difference.

Here's How We Measure Forgiveness:
1. *We think about who.* Who should we forgive? "She did this, and I don't know if I could forgive her." We think about the people involved. Do we really want to forgive them? We measure their value and question if they are worthy of our forgiveness.

2. *We think about how much.* We say to some things on our list, "No problem, I can forgive that." But sometimes we put our foot

down and say, "Hey, that's a bigger thing! I can't forgive that!" So we think about who it is; we keep track of how much they've done.

3. We think about how often. How's that saying go? "Fool me once, shame on you. Fool me twice, shame on me." We're like, "Nobody's going to do that to me again!" We measure everything. We measure who did it, how big the offense was and how often we were victimized.

4. We think about how many people. "If one person does it, I can let it go. But everybody has been running all over me; I have to put a stop to this!"

⑧ **Think about a time you had trouble forgiving an offense. Which of the following measures of forgiveness was the reason you had trouble forgiving? Check one.**
❏ a. Who   ❏ c. How often
❏ b. How much   ❏ d. How many people

We measure forgiveness with precision and puny capacity. I wonder if God shakes His head and says, "Your thoughts are so lame. They're so little. Look at Me and get the bigger picture."

The Bigger Picture of Forgiveness
We can't conceive God's boundaries on forgiveness. They're so much bigger and different than we can get into our heads. A man with a hundred billion dollars does not need to count pennies. So God, who is infinitely wealthy in forgiveness, doesn't measure or count it in any way. Think for a moment of all the people in all of human history and all the forgiveness God has granted to all the people. Can our minds even go that far? And since all our sin is ultimately against God, imagine all the times He has chosen to forgive. Isaiah is right—as high as the heavens are above the earth … and then double it … and again to infinity and beyond!

Charles Spurgeon said, "God's pardon is abundant because it wells up from an infinitely deep fountain. … Our sins may pile as high as the tallest mountains, but Jesus' blood, like Noah's flood, drowns them all."[1] Now that's abundant pardon!

Are you thinking, "God could never forgive me. If I ever brought my sin before the Lord, He would turn His back. I'm just going to have to carry this one myself. He's just not merciful enough to forgive me." My friend, you are so wrong! God can completely forgive everything.

⑨ **Is there something in your past for which you feel such guilt or shame you question whether God has forgiven you or even whether He could or would forgive you?** ❏ Yes ❏ No

Did you check yes? Then you need to be gripped by His abundant pardon. That's the whole point of God's greatness—His is a level of grace and forgiveness called "abundant pardon" that we struggle to comprehend. But it can be yours, even for that thing in your past.

But wait. Abundant pardon is not yours simply because it's been offered. It must be received and accepted. Perhaps you have never

> "Our sins may pile as high as the tallest mountains, but Jesus' blood, like Noah's flood, drowns them all."
>
> *Charles Spurgeon*

made the choice to claim God's forgiveness. You've seen others' lives changed, but your life hasn't changed. Why? Because you have never received God's abundant pardon.

In 1826, two men, last names Porter and Wilson, were sentenced to hang for robbing the U.S. Postal Service. Porter was hanged first in July 1830. Three weeks later, President Andrew Jackson pardoned Wilson, the second perpetrator. The death sentence was lifted.

Then the weirdest thing happened. Wilson refused the pardon saying, "I don't want the forgiveness." How bizarre! It sent the court system into confusion. What do we do? The President has pardoned and he doesn't want to be forgiven. The case took three years to resolve. It even went to the Supreme Court, where Justice John Marshall passed down an historic decision regarding the acceptance or rejection of a pardon. Here is what the Supreme Court said:

> "A pardon is a deed, to the validity of which, delivery is essential, and delivery is not complete, without acceptance. It may then be rejected by the person to whom it is tendered; and if it be rejected, we have discovered no power in a court to force it on him."[2]

Do you get how perfectly that parallels God's law? It doesn't matter how ready God is to pardon you if you will not accept it personally. If you will not embrace what God offers freely, if you won't by faith receive God's forgiveness, He won't force it on you.

🌿 **If you still need to accept God's abundant pardon for sin available to you because of Jesus' sacrifice, or if there still remains that one thing for which you've struggled to accept God's forgiveness, receive His forgiveness now. Talk to Him.**

⸺⸺⸺⸺∽∝∼⸺⸺⸺⸺

But to you who grasp the weight of the death sentence that our own sin truly deserves and then choose to be set free, you know what it's like to be gripped by the greatness of God! And you're smiling right now, because you know to whom all the credit goes. God is good!

⑩ **Read and meditate on David's description of abundant pardon and amazing grace in Psalm 103:2-5 in the margin. Picture yourself awash in the sea of God's forgiveness so unworthy but so abundantly pardoned. Ponder the greatness of that forgiveness and let it grip you.**

🌿 **Close today's study by writing in the margin a prayer of worship, praise, and thanksgiving for God's abundant pardon.**

Psalm 103:2-5

Bless the LORD, O my soul,
And forget none of His benefits;
Who pardons all your iniquities,
Who heals all your diseases;
Who redeems your life from
  the pit,
Who crowns you with lovingkindness
  and compassion;
Who satisfies your years with
  good things,
So that your youth is renewed
  like the eagle.

My Prayer:

DAY FOUR *Accomplished Truth & Absolute Delight*

🌿 Read Today's Walk in the Word verses in the margin, meditate on God's name, and talk to the Lord in prayer as you begin today's study.

IN GOD'S WORD WE FIND ACCOMPLISHED TRUTH

Understood only in the last few hundred years by scientists but written several thousands of years ago, the natural water cycle is explained in Isaiah 55:10-11. (Don't you love God's Word?) Rainwater doesn't just come down, it goes up again. God says, "My rain never comes down without accomplishing in the earth the purpose for which I send it down." In the very same sense, God makes a promise about His Word. That promise is in your memory verse.

① **Fill in the blanks for your Scripture memory verse this week:**

"'So will My _____ be which goes forth from My _____;

It will not _____ to Me _____, without

_____ what I _____, and without

_____ in the _____ for which I _____ it.'"

Every time a mother, father, pastor, small-group leader, or children's ministry worker speaks the Word of God, God says, "You think you're speaking, but what is really happening is that I'm sending forth My word through you." I just love verses 10 and 11.

Rain keeps us alive; it waters the earth, germinates seed, which produces bread to the eater, sustenance, and nourishment. But as good as that is, God's Word has an even better promise of return. "My Word will not return to Me empty." That's a 100 percent promise. Never will the Word of God go forth but that it will bear fruit. That is the work of God—so great in its extent that it can only grip our hearts in wonder. Everywhere around the world at this moment where God's Word is going forth, it has God's guarantee going with it. Something good is going to happen.

Parents, are you sowing the seed of God's Word into the hearts of your kids? God says, "Every time you sow that seed into the life of your child, it's going to bear fruit."

You say, "I go through days of doubting and weeks of wondering. I live and quote and memorize Scripture until they think I'm a walking

Today's Walk in the Word
2 Timothy 3:16-17—*"All Scripture is inspired by God and profitable for teaching, for reproof, for correction, for training in righteousness, so that the man of God may be adequate, equipped for every good work."*

Meditate on God's Name
The Word (John 1:1)
The Truth (John 14:6)

Talk to the Lord
Word of God, You are the Truth I need. Thank You for giving Scripture that I may know You and be taught by You. Thank You for the living Word that has power to accomplish all that You intend. Teach me from Your Word. Reprove and correct me. Train me in Your righteousness. Equip me for every good work that I may be complete and mature in my faith and usefulness to You. Amen.

Review Your Memory Verse
Isaiah 55:11—*"'So will My word be which goes forth from My mouth;*
It will not return to Me empty,
Without accomplishing what I desire,
And without succeeding in the matter for which I sent it.'"

Bible, and I just haven't seen the results." Listen. God says, "Don't worry about your part in that, I'm going to honor My Word."

② **Restate in your own words God's promise that the Word He sends out will accomplish His purposes for it.**

_____

_____

Right now we've got our noses in the book God wrote as we study Isaiah. God says, "Every time you open the pages of My Word and you speak My truth, I'm going to make sure it bears fruit." That's the only confidence that keeps me preaching every week.

I'll let you in on a pastor's secret. Sometimes we pastors get really, really tired of standing up with an open Bible in front of people with closed hearts. So why do we do it? The reason is right here in verses 10 and 11. If you sow the seed of God's Word into people's lives, God promises that He will accomplish what He desires to accomplish.

God's holy Word will always get results. God's commitment to His Word is one of His greatest works.

Maybe you're sharing Christ with someone at work or in your neighborhood. Maybe you're burdened for someone you love. Sow the seed of God's Word in his or her life. Drop your dependence on human persuasion. Sow the seed of God's Word. Scatter the seed and wait for the fruit. Drop all your clever arguments and persuasions and share the Word of God.

> God's commitment to His Word is one of His greatest works.

③ **In what ways will you sow the seed of God's Word into the lives of others? Check all that you will do or write your own.**
   ❏ a. Help my family read, meditate on, and study God's Word.
   ❏ b. Share truths from God's Word with friends or coworkers.
   ❏ c. Teach God's Word to children, youth, or adults at my church.
   ❏ d. Distribute Bibles or Scripture portions to people who need copies of God's Word to read for themselves.
   ❏ e. Other: _____

Staying Faithful

I struggled spiritually when I was in high school. At a time when I had just returned to the Lord and was trying to get my life back together, my youth pastor made me go to a conference. I didn't want to go, but looking back I see God was drawing me back to Himself.

The conference speaker was Tom Maharias from Manhattan Bible Church. He shared from Scripture why it was impossible for the character of Christ to grow in the life of a person whose mind was filled with worldly sewage. That was me. My whole life was polluted by the heavy-metal filth I had poured through my headphones in daily doses.

But now I had returned to the Lord. I was trying to go forward spiritually, but I was chained to something that was holding me back. Pastor Maharias challenged us with "Do you want the character of

Christ to grow in your mind? Then get the sewage out." He wisely pressed us to make a decision. He challenged us to stand up and make a public decision to put only Christ-honoring messages in our minds.

It was one of those times when I knew the Lord was speaking with me, so I stood up. I remember my body felt like lead. Out of several hundred young people, I was the only person to stand that day. The only one.

Twenty years later, I had the opportunity to meet Tom Maharias. I asked if he remembered the teen conference in Ontario, Canada. He said, "I remember that well. I was so discouraged. I preached my heart out and went home wondering if God did a single thing that day."

I said, "That day changed my life!"

If you're weary in doing the right thing, stay at it. You can trust that as the rains come and go, God is at work behind the scenes … growing His fruit to be ready for harvest in His time. Be faithful to sow the truth of His Word, and He promises that it will not return without succeeding in the purpose for which He sent it forth.

FINDING ABSOLUTE DELIGHT IN GOD'S WORKS

"For you will go out with joy and be led forth with peace; the mountains and the hills will break forth into shouts of joy before you, and all the trees of the field will clap their hands" (v. 12).

Even on the sunniest day, everything looks dull and hazy when your eyes are closed to the reality of your Creator God. But when your eyes are opened to the greatness of God's works, suddenly you hear birds singing and everything becomes beautiful. God's created world bursts into praise before your eyes! Suddenly your overwhelming desire is to join nature's chorus of worship to God! It's not just the trees and mountains that acknowledge the reality of their Designer. As the pinnacle of God's creation, we're supposed to be leading the band.

That's what verse 13 talks about. "Instead of the thorn bush [thorns were part of the curse in Genesis 3] the cypress will come up [a strong, useful life is pictured in that tree], and instead of the nettle the myrtle will come up, and it will be a memorial to the LORD." Isaiah says your life is a memorial to God. Your life is a testimony to the faithfulness and the greatness of God, "an everlasting sign which will not be cut off."

The picture here is of pure delight in God. "Listen carefully to Me, and eat what is good, and delight yourself in abundance" (v. 2). Hear that? Delight yourself in the great things of God! Enjoy them. Open your heart to what He's doing. Don't be afraid to look and laugh and love God's wonderful work.

🍃 **Close today's study by praising God for His wonderful works. If time and weather permit, go outside into a place where you can see some of God's glory in nature. Join with creation in praise to your Creator.**

> Be faithful to sow the truth of His Word, and He promises that it will not return without succeeding in the purpose for which He sent it forth.

DAY FIVE *Responding to God's Works*

Today's Walk in the Word
Psalm 63:1—*"O God, You are my God; I shall seek You earnestly; My soul thirsts for You, my flesh yearns for You, In a dry and weary land where there is no water."*

Meditate on God's Name
Fountain of Living Waters (Jeremiah 2:13)

Talk to the Lord
Fountain of Living Waters, spring up in my life. Satisfy my spiritual thirst for You. I've known periods of dryness, even spiritual draught. But I know You are more than sufficient to satisfy my every need. I pray that you will fill me with Yourself and quench my thirst. Lord, I am satisfied with You! Amen.

Write Your Memory Verse
Isaiah 55:11—

_____

_____

_____

_____

_____

_____

🌿 Read Today's Walk in the Word verse in the margin, meditate on God's name, and talk to the Lord in prayer.

① **What would it mean to you to want God as much as David, the psalmist, wanted Him in Psalm 63:1? Fill in the blanks:**

I desire Him like a _____ needs _____.

Don't Just Think It, Express Yourself!
I go to more than my share of funerals. Over the years I've witnessed hundreds of people stand and give testimonies of the one whose life they are celebrating. I've come to realize that in their expressions of love, their grief is overshadowed by joy. C. S. Lewis said that people don't have some incessant need to compliment but that people in love tell one another how beautiful they are because the joy is not complete without the expression.[3]

Until you say, "I love you," and "I thank God for you" to the loved ones in your life, your joy cannot be complete. And it's the same with God. If you know the Lord, then throughout this chapter there has been something welling up inside of you saying, "Yes! God is the God of satisfaction and abundant pardon! Yes! His Word does accomplish the purpose for which it is sent forth. Yes! My only delight can be found in Him!" His works are gripping, and I have to tell Him so.

You don't need a choir, guitar, or congregation to acknowledge the works of God. If your heart is gripped by the greatness of God's work, let your expression of praise be audible. And when it is … well, you'll see.

🌿 Stop and voice or sing your expression of joy, love, and delight to the Lord for His great works.

⊷⊶

② **Read Isaiah 55:1-13 in your Bible. Choose a verse, phrase, or word and ponder it. Ask questions of it. Pray over it. Write it in the margin. Look up other verses that use the same word. Look for at least one way you could apply it or live it. As you soak your soul slowly in the water of the Word, ask God to refresh you with it and prompt a thirst for more.**

If you long to know God and please Him and to grow in spiritual maturity, that's the work of God's grace in your soul. Be thankful for it. In your carnal state (your life before you were a believer in Christ Jesus), this wouldn't have been your desire. But when a person thirsts after God, it proves that God's Spirit is alive and active within him and he enjoys God's abundance.

③ **Read about God's provision for the hungry and thirsty soul in the Scriptures in the margin. Underline the words that describe what God will do.**

✎ **Ask God to make you more hungry and thirsty for Him. Tell Him of your desire to be filled with abundance, to drink His delights, to be satisfied, and to be filled with what is good.**

When you are gripped by the greatness of God's works, it fires you up to faithfulness. In fact, nothing is more essential to success in the Christian life than endurance, perseverance, keeping at it. Remembering God's work in your life will help you persevere.

④ **Take a trip down memory lane. Think of times or ways you have experienced the following and write notes on a separate sheet of paper to remind yourself of God's works in your life.**
   - **God's works bring complete satisfaction. Ask yourself, "Will I get that anywhere else?"**
   - **God provides abundant pardon. Ask yourself, "Who else promises forgiveness of sin and release from guilt?"**
   - **God's Word provides accomplished truth. Ask yourself, "Who else can accomplish everything He says He will?"**
   - **God's works produce absolute delight. Ask yourself, "Is there anything else that can give me real joy?"**

The answers to all these questions are found only in God. Stay faithful—it's worth it.

⑤ **Special assignment (for you or your small group): Seek out one or more people in your family or church who have walked with God for more than 50 years (someone like Roy on page 78). Invite them to coffee or to a meal. Ask them to share milestones of their spiritual journeys. Be alert to the factors that have shaped their faithfulness and begin building them into your life. Look for a way to honor them for their model of faithfulness.**

✎ **Close out this week's study by praying the closing prayer in the margin. Pray it slowly and make the prayer your own.**

[1] Tom Carter, compiler, *Spurgeon's Commentary on Great Chapters of the Bible* (Grand Rapids, MI: Kregel Publications, 1998), 87,88.
[2] John Marshall, United States v. George Wilson 32 U.S. 150, 7 Pet. 150, 8 L.Ed. 640 [cited 16 August 2005]. Available from the Internet: *www.jurisearch.com/newroot/caselink.asp?citationno=32+U.S.+150&series=USSC*
[3] C. S. Lewis, *Reflections on the Psalms* (New York: Harcourt, Brace and Company, 1958) 95.

Psalm 36:8— *"They drink their fill of the abundance of Your house; And You give them to drink of the river of Your delights."*

Psalm 107:9—*"For He has satisfied the thirsty soul, And the hungry soul He has filled with what is good."*

Matthew 5:6— *"Blessed are those who hunger and thirst for righteousness, for they shall be satisfied."*

Closing Prayer
Father, don't ever let me forget Your incredible works in my life—works that bring me satisfaction, abundant forgiveness, truth, and delight. Each one of them is gold. Keep me from embracing the temptation that anything apart from You could ever satisfy me. In the long, difficult days, restore my heart with the reminder of Your covenant love and mercy. Prompt me with every sunrise to remember Your faithfulness, renewable for eternity. I want to be faithful in return. Thank you for your work in my life. Help me never get over the greatness of Your works. Amen.

GRIPPED BY THE
GREATNESS
GOD OF

GRIPPED BY THE WORSHIP OF GOD

Follow the session plans in the leader's guide on page 141.

Discussion Guide on the Works of God

1. What have you learned or experienced about God's works this week that has been most meaningful or life changing?

2. What characteristics, attitudes, or behaviors did you identify in Roy's life that are worth imitating? (p. 78)

3. In small groups, describe your responses to activity 3 (p. 83) and activity 2 (p. 85). Then take time to pray for each other.

4. If you can identify with the experience of coming to Christ because a "boulder" dropped on you (activity 6, p. 88), describe your experience.

5. What are four ways we measure forgiveness (pp. 88-89), and which one do you think causes us the greatest difficulty in forgiving others? How can Christ help us?

6. What are some ways you want to sow the seed of God's Word into the lives of others? (activity 3, p. 92)

7. If you have interviewed an older saint (activity 5, p. 95), share your observations about their model of faithfulness.

DVD Message Notes on the Worship of God (21 minutes)

Worship: ascribe worth, express adoration to God

1. God ignores our worship when …
   a. we are _____, seeking our own pleasure.
   b. we are filled with _____.
   c. we are surface-y. God wants the reality, not just the symbol.

God's Spirit can grip your heart, if you meet the prerequisites.

2. God ignites our _____ when …
   a. we experience the _____ of Christ (Isa. 58:6, John 8:36).
   b. we express the _____ of Christ (Isa. 58:7)

   Four places we can show compassion
   - To the _____
   - To the naked (helpless)
   - To the homeless poor
   - To your own flesh (family)

Responding to the Message

1. For which reason do you believe God is most likely to ignore your worship (individually or as a church) and why?
2. What are some things you can do (individually and as a group) to increase the likelihood that God will ignite your worship?
3. What are some ways you can become involved through your church in showing compassion to others?

Preview Statements for This Week's Study

- God made us so that we could reflect His glory back to Him.
- Sin distances your heart from the Lord's abundant provision.
- You cannot have everything your heart desires and God!
- Fasting, as prescribed in Scripture, elevates our hunger and passion for God.
- As with most symbolic expressions of worship, over time the people became guilty of offering God the symbol and not the reality.
- God cares about people that no one else cares about: the hungry, the homeless, and the helpless.
- God won't meet you at church on Sunday if His ways have been banned from your home throughout the week.
- God's presence in response to sincere worship is the means to true victory.
- God's presence quickly stalls in a stingy heart.

This Week's Mountaintop in Isaiah—Isaiah 58:1-11 (Selected Verses)

[2] "They seek Me day by day and delight to know My ways, as a nation that has done righteousness and has not forsaken the ordinance of their God. They ask Me for just decisions, they delight in the nearness of God.

[3] 'Why have we fasted and You do not see? Why have we humbled ourselves, and You do not notice?' Behold, on the day of your fast you find your desire, and drive hard all your workers.

[5] "Is it a fast like this which I chose, a day for a man to humble himself? Is it for bowing one's head like a reed and for spreading out sackcloth and ashes as a bed? Will you call this a fast, even an acceptable day to the LORD?

[6] "Is this not the fast which I chose, to loosen the bonds of wickedness, to undo the bands of the yoke, and to let the oppressed go free and break every yoke?

[7] "Is it not to divide your bread with the hungry and bring the homeless poor into the house; when you see the naked, to cover him; and not to hide yourself from your own flesh?"

It Happened to Me

My wife and I began Harvest Bible Chapel in the late 1980s with a committed group of pioneers and a vision to see God powerfully at work.

By the time Harvest Bible Church was 13 years old, our weekly services were maxed out—we couldn't add any more services; we couldn't add any more parking. We needed to find new property. After two agonizing years, we uncovered a piece of land perfectly suited for our needs. Problem: The property was owned by the Catholic church and they don't sell much—especially not to an evangelical church. Nevertheless, our church's history is one of multiplied miraculous answers to prayer and so we set about to test the promises of God.

I filled my heart with faith and repeatedly went out on the property to walk and pray. Our elders gathered on the vacant land, calling out to God by faith and asking Him to give us this land.

Doors began to open. Key people within the ranks of the Catholic hierarchy began to soften to the idea of selling us the land. I continued to pray as the private negotiations accelerated. So focused I became on "claiming this mountain" that I hardly thought of anything else.

I begged God to do this work and put myself in a very dangerous position spiritually. We must be very careful of begging God to do some specific work in a way that quenches our thirst for Him and His greatness alone.

Praying and pleading for a specific something as I had been made me vulnerable. So, when the news came that we would not be getting the property, I faced a crisis in my own faith, finding it hard to understand why God would refuse the only possibility for our future that I could see.

Late in January 2003, we were made aware of a corporate building on 85 acres of land 20 miles from our church. We hadn't considered it before because it was outside our search area.

This property was owned by the Green family from Oklahoma City; you might know them as the owners of the Hobby Lobby store chain. The property included a 285,000 square foot building with a 900-car parking garage. It was purchased and built in 1993 at a cost of $53 million.

This property was available as a gift from the Greens to a ministry of their choice, with the specification that the property could not be resold, that the recipient must demonstrate a similarity of conviction and a readiness to bear the financial cost of developing the site into a meaningful center of gospel ministry.

The opportunity seemed perfect, but I determined in my heart I would never again get attached to a particular property as God's will for our church.

We flew to Oklahoma City and made our vision for the property known. We were told that we were in the final running for the property with Jerry Falwell of Liberty University. In February 2003, Dr. Falwell rang my cell phone. He introduced himself and said, "I understand you're interested in the Hobby Lobby property." "Yes," I answered with a shaky voice. "Well," he said, "we are flying down tomorrow and they are going to give the property to us."

I was glad I had been praying with an open heart, because the first words out of my mouth were a lot different than they would have been any other time. "That's good news for us, Dr. Falwell. We have been praying for God's will to be done; and, if that means the property is for you, then we can get on to whatever He has in store for us."

He asked me about our church and over the course of the conversation I sensed a subtle change in his tone. Suddenly he confessed, "I am 69 years old and have all I can handle here in Lynchburg. I think I'm going to tell them they ought to give the property to you." And that is exactly what he did.

Within a few days we received the news that the property was ours! Amazing, awesome provision of God. A $53 million dollar facility for our church for $1.

Hopefully you can avoid the painful valley of doubt that came to me as a result of wanting a specific work of God rather than His plan, His timing, His way.

Here's the lesson: God must be God, and He will be. Our choices are worshipful submission or stubborn rebellion. Choose to worship; choose words of praise and gratitude. Worship like that will find for you a fountain of joy reserved for those who want more than a simple surface faith. I can tell you that for sure, not just because I've seen it in others; but because it happened to me.

DAY ONE *Get a Grip on Your Worship of God*

🖊 Read Today's Walk in the Word verse in the margin, meditate on God's name, and talk to the Lord in prayer as you begin.

① Isaiah 58:2 (Today's Walk in the Word) describes a way we can worship the Lord. I want you to memorize it this week. Begin now by filling in the blanks below.

" 'They _____ Me day by day and _____ to know

My _____, As a _____ that has done _____,

And has not _____ the _____

of their God. They ask Me for just _____,

They _____ in the _____ of God.' "

The Glory of God

Isaiah 43:7 says, "I have created [you] for My glory, … I have formed [you]." God made us so that we could reflect His glory back to Him. Glory is what emanates from God. Although we can't see God (1 John 4:12), we can see His glory in creation and in His people when they model His holiness. Glory is the evidence that God is present.

God's purpose is to bring glory to Himself or display Himself in you. He wants to bring Himself glory even in the most mundane things. "Whatever you do, do all to the glory of God" (1 Cor. 10:31).

② **Read 1 Corinthians 10:31 in the margin and circle the word describing *how much* we are to do for His glory.**

③ **How would you rate the amount of God's glory that shines through your life? How do you think others would rate it? Write *M* for Me and *O* for Others beside your choices.**
____ a. It's surely a miracle! People comment about seeing God in my life. That's His glory and nothing of me.
____ b. No glory here. People wouldn't even see a glimmer in me.
____ c. Sundays I'm shining. Mondays I'm pretty dim.
____ d. God's work in my life shines in a number of places, praise the Lord. But I've got some areas that need more work.
____ e. Other _____

_____

Today's Walk in the Word
Isaiah 58:2—*" 'They seek Me day by day and delight to know My ways, As a nation that has done righteousness And has not forsaken the ordinance of their God. They ask Me for just decisions, They delight in the nearness of God.' "*

Meditate on God's Name
The Father of glory
(Ephesians 1:17)

Talk to the Lord
Dear Father of glory, I do delight to know Your ways. I delight in Your nearness, but I confess that my worship is sometimes flat. Teach me to experience true worship that pleases You. Grip me this week with new dimensions of Your greatness. Amen.

GLORY
What emanates from God, the evidence that God is present

1 Corinthians 10:31—*"Whether, then, you eat or drink or whatever you do, do all to the glory of God."*

Where's the Action?

OK, you've read this far and that means you really want to be gripped by the reality of God's greatness. But if you're a person who likes action, you may be saying to yourself, *Learning, learning, learning. Isn't there something for me to **do**?* Yes! Worship the way this chapter explains, and I absolutely guarantee almighty God will grip you with His greatness.

You ask, "James, how can you possibly know what God will do for me?" Because I know what He has promised. In fact, I am so sure about this that I am going to press you very hard to take action. I am going to push you to get out of your comfort zone. Look at the passion God invited Isaiah to express on this all important subject: "Cry loudly, do not hold back; raise your voice like a trumpet, and declare to My people" (v. 1). In other words,

Say it now and say it loud!

"Now don't get so worked up," some people might say. "God's Word should be taught in a calm, cool, careful manner." If the world can shout trash and trivia all day, certainly God's people can get fired up about what the Creator commands and calls us to do. We don't have to hold back. What's our message?

④ **Read verse 1 (in the margin) again and <u>underline</u> what Isaiah was to declare to God's people.**

Don't Be Afraid!

When you read the word *transgression* or *sin*, you probably thought you were gonna get blasted, right? Wrong! That is neither the content nor the tone of what God inspired Isaiah to say. It's more like the prophet is pleading: "Listen, precious one. More than you could even comprehend, it's your sin that keeps you from the incredible grace and greatness of God. Sin distances your heart from the Lord's abundant provision for you. Please don't deny or defend. I beg you to open your heart and begin to honestly address this issue."

⑤ **Which of the following best describes the tone of verse 1?**
   ❏ a. A loving Father wanting to train a child
   ❏ b. An angry taskmaster ready to whip a slave

God is speaking more like the loving Father. Far from condemnation, Isaiah invites us into joyful transformation. Picture Isaiah coming to you and saying, "That sin in your life? It's keeping you from wealth you can't imagine. But if you face it and forsake it, God will put stuff in its place that will blow you away!"

"Yeah, yeah. I've heard all this before. God does it for others, I'm sure, but not for me."

Isaiah 58:1—" '*Cry loudly,*
   do not hold back;
Raise your voice like a trumpet,
And declare to My people
   their transgression.' "

TRANSGRESSION
overstepping the limit,
breaking the law

Sin distances
your heart from
the Lord's abundant
provision for you.

⑥ **Do you feel like that? Does it seem like others always experience God in ways that pass you by? Do you observe others being gripped and wonder why it's not happening to you? Check your response.**
❏ a. Yes. Never happens to me.
❏ b. No. I've experienced the Lord's goodness many times.
❏ c. Sometimes I sense Him near and sometimes I don't.

You may feel like God is playing some cosmic game of "hide and seek." You look for Him in your Bible and at church and through service but at times you're tempted to say "Come out, come out, wherever You are." If this describes your experience, you need to know that this longing you have is a real thing. You are seeking and in a way God is hiding. The people in Isaiah's day felt like that, too.

⑦ **Read Isaiah 58:1-3 in the margin and <u>underline</u> the two questions God's people were asking.**

Verse 3 describes a common complaint among God's people: "We've humbled ourselves and You don't notice." In other words, "Lord, why does it seem that I do the things I am supposed to in order to connect with You, and You completely ignore me?"

A man in our church recently said to me, "I come every week. I sit in the right seat. I hold the right book in my hands. I sing the right words to the right songs, but I am just going through the motions! God is not showing up in my life." Ever feel like that? Tomorrow I am going to show you from Scripture why that happens. But let me start by saying, it does happen! You're not alone, and there is help!

🖋 **Close today's study with a time of prayer. Tell God what you are feeling about your relationship with Him. Thank Him for blessings. Confess to Him your desires and any confusion you may feel. Ask Him to reveal what you need this week to ignite genuine worship in your heart. Write your prayer below.**

_____

_____

_____

_____

_____

_____

Isaiah 58:1-3—*"Declare to My people their transgression. Yet they seek Me day by day and delight to know My ways, As a nation that has done righteousness And has not forsaken the ordinance of their God. They ask Me for just decisions, They delight in the nearness of God. Why have we fasted and You do not see? Why have we humbled ourselves and You do not notice?"*

DAY TWO *When God Ignores Our Worship*

Today's Walk in the Word
Psalm 102:2— *"Do not hide
Your face from me in the day
of my distress;
Incline Your ear to me;
In the day when I call answer
me quickly."*

Meditate on God's Name
God who sees (Genesis 16:13)

Talk to the Lord
Lord, You are a God who sees
and hears. Like the psalmist,
I beg You not to hide Your
face from me. Watch over
me. Listen to me. Speak; I'm
listening. When I call, answer
me. Reveal to me anything that
would hinder me from such a
relationship with You. Amen.

Review Your Memory Verse
Isaiah 58:2— *" 'They seek Me
day by day and delight
to know My ways,
As a nation that has done
righteousness
And has not forsaken the
ordinance of their God.
They ask Me for just decisions,
They delight in the nearness
of God.' "*

Read Today's Walk in the Word verse in the margin, meditate on God's name, and talk to the Lord in prayer as you begin.

If it seems like God is keeping His distance and sort of ignoring your attempts to draw near to Him, He might be. Let's consider why God might be holding you at arm's length even as you're seeking Him.

REASON #1: OUR WORSHIP IS SELFISH.

" 'Behold, on the day of your fast you find your desire, and drive hard all your workers' " (v. 3). That phrase "find your desire" means you already have pretty much everything you want. Often when we come to worship, we're basically satisfied with everything our hearts desire. Then we rush into church almost as an afterthought and say by our actions, "Oh yeah, God; I want You, too." Sorry, it doesn't work that way. You cannot have everything your heart desires and God!

If you doubt that, try a little experiment. Set this book down and go eat a big meal. In fact, eat it in front of the TV while you watch a movie. If possible, choose a film that shows total disrespect for the things of God. When you're done eating, lay down on the couch as the movie continues. When the movie is over, come back to this book and see how much energy and desire you have to study about worship. The answer will be little or none. Creeping up in the back of your mind as you try to read is a sense of futility or even hypocrisy.

① **Read Isaiah 29:13 and Deuteronomy 4:29 in the margin on page 103. Which one more nearly describes your regular experience of worship these days? Check one or describe your worship.**
   ❑ a. Isaiah 29:13. I have to confess, I'm just going through the motions in worship; but I don't have a heart of worship.
   ❑ b. Deuteronomy 4:29. I've really been seeking the Lord and He's faithful. I've been experiencing Him in worship.
   ❑ c. _____

Deep down we know we cannot have God and the constant satisfaction of every earthly whim. As obvious as that seems, most Christians believe that only sin hinders their relationship with God. That's why Isaiah focuses on fasting. Fasting, as prescribed in Scripture, elevates our hunger and passion for God.

Spending our energy to satisfy our flesh inevitably creates apathy toward God. I believe that's why there is so much spiritual shallowness in the Western World. We think our material blessings are a sign of

God's favor upon us. Wrong! Maybe it's time we honestly recognized financial prosperity for what it often is: not so much a blessing from God but the result of having systematically neglected the priority of our relationship with Him.

This phrase, "you find your desire," is God's way of saying you can't have your cake and eat it too! Remember Jesus words: "Blessed are those who hunger and thirst for righteousness, because they will be filled" (Matt. 5:6, HCSB). It seems you can only be filled when you have an empty place to hold what God longs to give you. Bottom line: God won't be hurried, and He's not your hobby. God will be your hunger or nowhere to be found!

🌿 **Take a break to think about your hunger for God. If it's not what God desires, ask Him what kind of fasting (doing without) you could do to increase your hunger for Him. Think about some of the options listed in the margin and check any you decide to try.**

Secondly, God doesn't show up in your worship because " 'you drive ... your workers' " (v. 3). When you are on the job, are you nice to the people you work with? If you or your spouse have employees, are they rewarded for loyalty and hard work; or do you squeeze them for every nickel you can make? Do you fight to see that company profits are equitably distributed, or do you support a system that gives more to those who need it least? God cares very deeply about these matters of justice. We can't ignore this subject and then act surprised if God ignores our worship. He will only grip our hearts with the joy of His presence when we seek Him on His terms—"a God of truth and without iniquity, just and right is he" (Deut. 32:4, KJV).

Next time you feel like a wallflower at a worship service, watching others' enthusiasm and wondering why you can't seem to enter in, ask yourself honestly *Am I selfish? Have I been consumed with what will meet my needs, even at the expense of others? Is God just another item on my "feel good" list?* If yes, we must not be surprised if God shakes His head and says, "Go ahead, do your thing. But don't expect Me to be part of it." God is 24/7/365 in the midst of all we are and do—or He won't show up at all.

② **What is one reason God ignores your worship?**

He ignores my worship when I am _____.

REASON #2: WE ARE STRIFE-FILLED.

Christians can sometimes be directionally challenged. Some are consumed with the vertical and think they can avoid or ignore horizontal relationships. You may have some horizontal stuff (with people) that you need to deal with before you can get the vertical thing right

Isaiah 29:13—" 'These people approach Me with their mouths to honor Me with lip–service— yet their hearts are far from Me, and their worship [consists of] man–made rules learned [by rote]' " (HCSB).

Deuteronomy 4:29—" 'You will seek the LORD your God, and you will find Him if you search for Him with all your heart and all your soul.' "

"Fasting" to Increase My Hunger
- ❑ Skip a meal (or more) to take time to pray
- ❑ Turn off the television for a week and spend more time in Bible study, prayer, listening to Christian radio, or reading a biography of a hero of faith
- ❑ Take a half-day or whole day away from routines to get away with the Lord in prayer and meditation
- ❑ Intentionally replace some time normally spent on pleasure or recreation to get together with Christian friends and do something for someone else
- ❑ Take a holiday, vacation day, or other day off work to minister to a needy person, family, or group
- ❑ Take a weekend or a week to go on a mission trip

with God. Notice verse 4 says, " 'Behold, you fast for contention and strife and to strike with a wicked fist.' " In other words, you fuss and fume and fight with people all week and then you come to worship God. Instead of leaving church determined to get right with people and be an instrument of reconciliation in this world, you walk out and crab at the kids all the way home.

In the middle of all of that, you try to fold in some genuine, personal relationship with God. God is saying, "You're kidding, right? You want Me to connect with you when you're like this?" God doesn't meet with us when our lives are filled with strife.

Amazingly, a lot of Christians still think they can be right with God, i.e., vertically, when they have not done the horizontal work of seeking to be right with others. God has taught me the hard way that you can't have the vertical thing right with Him if you haven't at least done your part to make the horizontal relationships right.

Paul tells us, "If possible, so far as it depends on you, be at peace with all men" (Rom. 12:18). Jesus says in Matthew 5:23-24 that if you come to worship God and while you're at the altar you remember a problem you have with somebody, you should leave your sacrifice and go make the relationship right. Just get up and walk out, get on the phone or write the letter or get in your car and get over to that house. Humble yourself before that person and say, "I'm so sorry for what's happened. Please forgive me."

This sometimes involves matters that are very complex. Believe me, I know. When two followers of Christ see a difficult situation differently, reconciliation becomes extremely challenging. We are not to compromise the truth or make "peace at all cost." What we are commanded to do is to humble ourselves, admit the wrong we have done, and leave the rest with the Lord. When we have not made every effort we can to be right with others, God ignores our worship.

③ **Take a relationship check-up. Have you offended anyone and not gone to that person to get things right? Has anyone offended you and you are holding on to unforgiveness, anger, or bitterness? Think through the relationships in the margin and make a list on a separate sheet of paper of any broken relationships that come to mind.**

④ **Write in your own words a new title for this second reason God may ignore your worship.**

_____

REASON #3: WE ARE SURFACE-Y.

We may look really sincere. We may make all the right moves, but God ignores our worship when we're focused on externals. You can see this in verse 5: " 'Is it a fast like this which I choose? ... Is it for bowing one's head like a reed?' " In other words, did God ask that you bow low to the ground like some cattails on a windy day?

> God doesn't meet with us when our lives are filled with strife.

Relationships That May Need Reconciliation
- spouse
- child
- parent
- relative
- neighbor
- friend
- pastor
- elder or deacon
- church leader
- fellow Christian
- coworker
- boss
- employee
- business owner
- customer
- government official
- competitor
- doctor, attorney, or other professional

" 'And for spreading out sackcloth and ashes as a bed?' " (v. 5). Sackcloth was a coarse cloth made of goats' hair. Think of burlap. In the Old Testament, people who wanted to show that they were really serious with God wore this abrasive, rough clothing against their skin as a symbolic expression of their heartfelt brokenness. Then to make themselves even more uncomfortable, they would dump ashes on their heads. By radically rejecting all matters related to external appearance, they pictured a consuming concern for their hearts.

As with most symbolic expressions of worship, over time the people became guilty of offering God the symbol and not the reality. They came to worship decked out in burlap and soot but they failed to let the reality of their sinfulness penetrate their own hearts. God was saying, "Do you think that's where I'm at? Don't give Me the symbol; give Me the reality!"

⑤ **Let's talk about some contemporary equivalents. Read the following list of symbolic worship activities that are not genuine and check ones of which you've been guilty.**
   ❑ a. What if you raise your hands to God, a symbol of sincerity and purity—not out of a heightened sense of God's presence in your worship but just because the music is climaxing or because the person beside you does?
   ❑ b. What if you kneel to pray but on the inside you refuse to yield to what He has been pursuing and convicting you about?
   ❑ c. How about sitting in church with your Bible open but your heart closed?
   ❑ d. Or rushing to Bible study with a proud and unreachable spirit?
   ❑ e. Worst of all, how do you think God feels when we casually take the communion bread and cup? Imbibing the symbols of our most precious realities even as our minds wander to trivia and fail to seriously scour the hearts Christ died to cleanse?

⑥ **Describe this third reason in your own words.**

_____

God ignores our worship when we come thinking "what's in this for me?" ... when we come with broken relationships, ... when we do the externals, but our hearts are far from God. So many people feel frustrated that their worship is mere ritual, formula, and futility. Sadly, when we sing in this frame of mind, God puts His fingers in His ears. But it doesn't have to be like that. Tomorrow we'll study the kind of worship God ignites!

🍃 **Close today's study with a time of prayer. Tell God what your worship has been like recently. Confess any ways your worship has not measured up to His standard. Express your hunger and thirst for more of Him. Ask Him to give you a new heart full of worship for Him in all His greatness.**

> Over time the people became guilty of offering God the symbol and not the reality.

DAY THREE *When God Ignites Our Worship*

WORSHIP

Today's Walk in the Word
Psalm 95:6 —*"Come, let us worship and bow down, Let us kneel before the LORD our Maker."*

Meditate on God's Name
Father of mercies and God of all comfort (2 Corinthians 1:3)

Talk to the Lord
Lord, my Maker. I do want to worship and bow down. I do want you to ignite my worship. I want it to be real. Speak to me today. Teach me to worship. Amen.

Review Your Memory Verse
Isaiah 58:2—*" 'They seek Me day by day and delight to know My ways, As a nation that has done righteousness, And has not forsaken the ordinance of their God. They ask Me for just decisions, They delight in the nearness of God.' "*

🍃 **Read Today's Walk in the Word verse in the margin, meditate on God's name, and talk to the Lord in prayer as you begin.**

If you've been a Christian long, you've probably known times when your worship was flat. You've likely also known times when God has shown up in wonderful, glorious ways and rocked your world.

① **How long has it been since you experienced His presence this way—when His greatness gripped your heart and broke you down, but it built you up, too? Describe below your most recent memory of gripping worship.**

_____

_____

WHEN WE EXPERIENCE THE FREEDOM OF CHRIST

You say, "That's what I want all the time!" Not wanting this to be a mystery, God laid out the details to Isaiah about when He will show up to powerfully ignite our worship with His awesome presence. God ignites our worship when we experience the freedom of Christ.

In Isaiah 58:6, God describes His kind of worship. He says, " 'Is this not the fast which I choose? To loosen the bonds of wickedness, to undo the bands of the yoke, and to let the oppressed go free and break every yoke?' " That phrase "bonds of wickedness" is a picture of a person who is chained to sin.

Do you know what it's like to be chained to sin? I do. Do you know what it's like to be chained to anger, deceit, lust, or greed? Try as you might to get free and live the way God wants you to live, somehow it just doesn't happen. Like some beast who stepped on a trap in the forest, you feel unable to get free. But in verse 6, Isaiah looks ahead to the ministry of Christ and pictures freedom that's for everyone.

Christ has come " 'to undo the bands of the yoke.' " A yoke is that huge wooden beam that binds two oxen together when they plow, or two horses when they pull. Wherever they go, they go together. Sometimes we're like that with sin. It seems no matter how hard we pull and fuss and even run to escape, we cannot get away from certain sins in our lives. Wherever we go, it goes with us!

What's that thing in your life right now? The good news of the gospel can break that yoke and give that sin the shove once and for all.

② **To illustrate your freedom from sin, draw the symbol for NO (⊘) on top of the chains and yoke in the margins.**

When we come together to worship God, we're coming together to celebrate the freedom Christ died and rose again to provide. When we are experiencing that in our lives, we can say, "I may not be perfect or have it together totally; but by God's grace, I've had some real victory this week. The bondage of sin has been broken in my life. The yoke has been thrown off. I'm experiencing true freedom, and it comes from my relationship with Christ."

God sees people sincerely worshiping Him and says, "When you get a group of people together who are experiencing the freedom only I can bring, I'll be there in the middle of that party, for sure!" The apostle Paul and Jesus echo Isaiah's cry for freedom.

③ **Read Galatians 5:1 and John 8:36 in the margin. Circle the words *freedom* and *free* each time they appear.**

④ **What is one reason God ignites your worship?** He ignites my

worship when I experience the _____.

🔖 **Stop to think about sins for which you've been forgiven and set free and thank God for the freedom from guilt and sin.**

Galatians 5:1—"It was for freedom that Christ set us free; therefore keep standing firm and do not be subject again to a yoke of slavery."

John 8:36— "So if the Son makes you free, you will be free indeed."

〜〜⬥〜〜

WHEN WE EXPRESS THE COMPASSION OF CHRIST

God also ignites our worship when we express the compassion of Christ. Now the issue moves from character on the inside to behavior on the outside. In other words, if you're experiencing freedom on the inside, it's going to show up in your actions.

⑤ **Read Isaiah 58:7 in the margin and write on the lines below the four kinds of people to whom we can show compassion.**

_____   _____

_____   _____

Isaiah 58:7— "Is it not to divide your bread with the hungry And bring the homeless poor into the house; When you see the naked, to cover him; And not to hide yourself from your own flesh?"

Isaiah lists four compassions which confirm the reality of Christ in our lives. God is looking for worship (fasting) that expresses itself in compassion for the hungry, homeless poor, naked, and your own flesh (or family). As you read the following sections, pray about ways God may want you to show compassion to those around you.

1. Compassion for the Hungry

If you read the Bible, you can't avoid God's heart for the hungry. Sadly though, we fall way short of implementing His orders. To help the hungry doesn't mean, "I have plenty, here's a little bit from my overflow." True biblical compassion gives to meet needs until it actually involves personal sacrifice.

I'll be honest. I don't know a lot about that depth of compassion. But I am very convinced that when we give with that kind of sacrifice we reflect God's heart. We can't close our hearts to the needs of the world and expect God to grip us in our worship (Prov. 21:13).

Proverbs 21:13— *"He who shuts his ear to the cry of the poor Will also cry himself and not be answered."*

⑥ **Write one people group to whom you can show compassion.**

naked (or helpless)	homeless poor
	flesh (or family)

2. Compassion for the Homeless Poor

God says, " 'This is the fast that I've chosen … To bring the homeless poor into the house.' " Isaiah isn't standing there with a bucket asking for your spare change. He's not telling you to send a check so that someone in Cleveland or Cambodia can have a roof over their heads (though that's a good thing to do). It's not even about picking up a homeless person in your car and taking him to the rescue mission. It's more like allowing someone with massive needs to come and stay with you and sticking with him until his life is back on track. That's compassion. That's when God says, "I'm showing up in your life powerfully and often."

Early in our marriage the Lord taught Kathy and me a lesson about this kind of sacrifice. The first person to live with us was a needy college student named Pam. She had no one to turn to in a rather large city and had known Kathy a little bit during their high school days. She was estranged from her family and seemed to be open to learning about the Lord. For many months Kathy and I shared our little home and our "newlywed" evenings with Pam. We brought her to church with us and pressed her consistently about the claims of Christ.

That was many years ago. I am not even sure where Pam is today, but I do know she was the first in a steady stream of people who have enriched our lives, impacted our children, and had their lives affected by living in our home. Rebellious teens, couples on the verge of divorce, lonely people looking for a place to be known and loved have filled our lives with God's kind of joy. Best of all, I believe that the Lord's grace in our lives, our abiding sense of His presence, and an almost continuous outpouring of abundance and blessing are directly related to these decisions of compassion—proof to us that " 'losing your life' " for the sake of others is a sure way to find it (Matt. 16:25).

" 'Losing your life' " for the sake of others is a sure way to find it

Matthew 16:25— *" 'Whoever wishes to save his life will lose it; but whoever loses his life for My sake will find it.' "*

⑦ **Write a second group to whom you can show compassion.**

hungry	
naked (or helpless)	flesh (or family)

3. Compassion for the Naked

Remember, God cares about people that no one else cares about: the hungry, the homeless, and the helpless. " 'When you see the naked … cover him' " (v. 7). That nakedness is a picture of helplessness. Rather than seeing a naked person and saying, "Tsk-tsk! How immodest!" God calls us to recognize the need and do all we can to meet it. It always amazes me that parents who want so much for their kids to embrace the gospel are so slow to see that living it out in practical, compassionate ways before their eyes is the strongest message of all. " 'In the same way, let your light shine before men, so that they may see your good works and give glory to your Father in heaven' " (Matt. 5:16).

⑧ **Write a third group to whom you can show compassion.**

hungry   homeless poor
_____   flesh (or family)

4. Compassion on the Home Front (Your Own Flesh)

Isaiah continues to define compassion: " 'Not to hide yourself from your own flesh.' " "Own flesh" is a reference to your family. Not the people in your church or on your street, but the people who sleep under your roof at night. At my graduation ceremony, Chuck Swindoll shared a message entitled, "Five Things They Never Taught Me in Seminary." I've never forgotten one of his points. He said, "It's hardest at home." As hard as it is to pick up a homeless person or feed a hungry person, the hardest place to live out the truth of the gospel is at home.

How many men sit in church week after week next to their emotionally starved wives? How many wives wonder why God won't answer their prayers yet are blind to the ways they continuously reject the protective covering God has provided in their own husbands? I know many heartbroken parents long for a genuine word of appreciation from their children (especially their adult children). God won't meet you at church on Sunday if His ways have been banned from your home throughout the week.

God's grace and God's strength are available for whatever your family needs. If we're not sincerely trying to apply these truths, then it's not right for us to wonder why God doesn't manifest Himself more obviously in our own individual or corporate worship.

⑨ **Write a fourth group to whom you can show compassion.**

hungry   homeless poor
naked (or helpless)   _____

🍂 **Close today's study with a time of prayer. Reflect on your need to experience the freedom of Christ and to express the compassion of Christ. Ask God what He wants you to do as a response to today's lesson and when. Write it in the margin. If names are attached to His directions, write them too.**

> God won't meet you at church on Sunday if His ways have been banned from your home throughout the week.

DAY FOUR *Worship Looks Like This*

Today's Walk in the Word

1 Chronicles 16:25-31—*"Great
is the LORD, and greatly
to be praised;
He also is to be feared above
all gods.
For all the gods of the peoples
are idols,
But the LORD made the heavens.
Splendor and majesty are
before Him,
Strength and joy are in His place.
Ascribe to the LORD, O families
of the peoples,
Ascribe to the LORD glory and
strength.
Ascribe to the LORD the glory
due His name;
Bring an offering, and come
before Him;
Worship the LORD in holy array.
Tremble before Him, all the earth;
Indeed, the world is firmly
established, it will not be moved.
Let the heavens be glad, and let
the earth rejoice;
And let them say among the
nations, 'The LORD reigns.'"*

Meditate on God's Name

The Light of the world (John 8:12)

Talk to the Lord

O Lord, You are great and
worthy of praise. I do worship
You, and I rejoice. I am in awe
of Your glory! I'm awfully glad
You reign. Amen.

🖋 **Read Today's Walk in the Word verses in the margin, meditate on God's name, and talk to the Lord in prayer as you begin.**

Beginning in verse 8, God is telling us that when you choose the fast He chooses, when you worship the way He wants to be worshiped, when you experience the freedom of Christ and minister the compassion of Christ, then when you get together for worship—get set! Isaiah 58 describes five different ways we know God is igniting our worship with Himself.

① **Read Isaiah 58:8-9 below and see if you can identify the five things God promises. Underline key words or write your own words beside the verses.**

> "Then your light will break out like the dawn,
> And your recovery will speedily spring forth;
> And your righteousness will go before you;
> The glory of the LORD will be your rear guard.
> Then you will call, and the LORD will answer;
> You will cry, and He will say, 'Here I am.'"

You may focus on different phrasing, but here's what I see: (1) your light will shine; (2) recovery, healing, health, and wholeness will come; (3) righteousness—victory over sin will be yours; (4) the Lord will protect you; (5) and when you need Him, He will be present.

#1 LIGHT

Many verses in the Bible describe a dynamic, personal relationship with God as light and a believer who lives in fellowship with God as walking in God's light. I can't explain God's light to you. I just know the Bible refers to it over and over again. When Moses came down from Mount Sinai, his face glowed (Ex. 34:29). When Jesus was transfigured before the disciples, "His face shone like the sun" (Matt. 17:2). How appropriate then that Christ promises that "the righteous will shine forth as the sun in the kingdom of their Father" (Matt. 13:43).

Notice Isaiah said that your light will "break out." Have you ever been up before dawn, perhaps on a night when some crisis robbed you of sleep? For hours the world is shrouded in darkness, then suddenly the black horizon begins to turn colors and—pow!—the sun breaks through! When God shows up in your life, light spills over from your life into a dark world. God's glory, the evidence of His presence, shines in us as we engage in genuine worship. Jesus even said, " 'You [plural] are the light of the world' " (Matt. 5:14).

② **Fill in the blank to make the following statement true.**
When God's light is shining in the lives of His people,

we are the _____ of the world.

#2 RECOVERY

" 'Your recovery will speedily spring forth' " (v. 8). The word *recovery* means wholeness or health. God's presence in response to our sincere worship brings recovery. Do you need physical healing? Do you have some scars from the past that your wounded heart won't let rest? The promise here is that "your recovery will speedily spring forth." We see many shysters in the church today who promise physical healing and set their hopeful audience up for shame and disappointment.

Then there are those who relegate the healing ministry of Christ to a "different dispensation." Hiding their lack of faith behind their theological system, they keep God's people from experiencing the healing God does want to bring. God does heal, not on demand and not in every circumstance; but He does heal both physically and emotionally. Between those two extremes is the historic consensus of the church of Jesus Christ: God heals.

🍃 **Pause to talk to the Lord about any area of your life where you need His healing touch, whether emotional or physical. Pray that He will restore wholeness and health. Consider asking a brother or sister in Christ to pray with and for you.**

———————⨳———————

If you need healing in mind or in body, remember that unless God's power is revealed, neither is possible. The recovery God brings comes through His manifest presence in response to sincere worship.

#3 RIGHTEOUSNESS

" 'And your righteousness will go before you' " (v. 8). In moments of real honesty, most believers will admit to the pain of battling certain, "besetting sins." Why do I keep doing that? When will I ever get victory over this? Will this always be a struggle for me?

God says, "When I show up in response to your worship, you have the power to conquer that thing that is keeping you down." Maybe victory over sin has been more absent than present in your life. That can change!

As 2 Corinthians 2:14 says, "Thanks be to God, who always leads us in triumph in Christ, and manifests through us the sweet aroma of the knowledge of Him in every place." This verse pictures a Roman victory parade. God, the conquering warrior, has defeated our

Review Your Memory Verse
Isaiah 58:2—" 'They seek Me
    day by day and delight
    to know My ways,
As a nation that has done
    righteousness
And has not forsaken the
    ordinance of their God.
They ask Me for just decisions,
They delight in the nearness
    of God.' "

enemies and leads those of us who have been "taken captive by Christ" to His home. At the head of this victory parade, incense is burned—and its strong fragrance, here compared to the knowledge of Christ, blows everywhere. When we allow God's righteousness to reign in our lives, we belong to a new king. Just as that incense spreads, we begin to see change and growth and transformation in our lives.

Romans 6:6-7—*"Our old self was crucified with Him, in order that our body of sin might be done away with, so that we would no longer be slaves to sin; for he who has died is freed from sin."*

③ **Read Romans 6:6-7,14 in the margin and describe below how much control sin has in your life when Christ dwells there.**

_____

_____

Romans 6:14—*"Sin shall not be master over you, for you are not under law but under grace."*

These are all things God wants to do for you. But you can't get victory in your own strength. You can't become a different person out of sheer willpower because you say, "I'm not doing that anymore!" Romans 8:8 says that "those who are in the flesh cannot please God." God's presence in response to sincere worship is the means to true victory.

> God's presence in response to sincere worship is the means to true victory.

#4 PROTECTION

" 'The glory of the LORD will be your rear guard' " (v. 8). *Rear guard* is a military term. When God led the children of Israel out of Egypt, He led them with a pillar of fire. But when they got through the Red Sea, the pillar went around behind them and protected them so their enemies would not recapture their victory ground (Ex. 14:19).

God says, "I want our victories to last forever!" No more winning the battle but losing the war. God's presence in response to sincere worship protects us from going retro. No more short-lived successes, only permanent victory because of Him!

🖋 **In what area are you most in need of God's protection as a "rear guard"? Tell the Lord about your desire to continue walking in victory in that area. If you are yet to win victory there, ask the Lord to bring you through to victory.**

#5 PRESENCE

" 'Then you will call, and the LORD will answer; you will cry, and He will say, "Here I am" ' " (v. 9). Isn't that the kind of walk with God we all long for? I call and He answers quickly with the comforting affirmation, "Here I am." He promises Himself, His presence.

TWO RULES

I talk to so many Christians who are aggravated that God has not done some of the things He promised in their lives. Often there is a reason God has not answered. They have to meet God's conditions. Yet, they still insist on doing the Christian life their own way, refusing to come to God on the terms He has laid down so clearly and repeatedly. God promises to do great things in our lives, but He reminds us of the rules of the game.

The first rule requires an honest look at yourself—" 'If you remove the yoke from your midst, the pointing of the finger and speaking wickedness' " (v. 9). The yoke Isaiah is talking about is the yoke of sin. We must eliminate all known sin both in attitude and action. We must repent of the ways we have failed the Lord and seek His grace to begin again. The pointing finger pictures our attitudes toward others. The feelings of superiority we quietly nurture in our garden of pride. The critical comments, thought or spoken, that tear others down. Get rid of them.

Get rid of sin and wrong attitudes toward others. "Give yourself to the hungry and satisfy the desire of the afflicted" (v. 10). The second rule is to be willing to meet the needs of those around us as often as we can. God's presence quickly stalls in a stingy heart. If we are generous and quick to share what we have with those who have not, only then can we expect the delight of the manifest presence and power of God.

④ **Why might God not be showing up and keeping His promises when you worship? Check any that apply.**
   ❏ a. I haven't put away all known sin.
   ❏ b. I hold on to critical attitudes toward others.
   ❏ c. I've been stingy and refused to help those in need around me.

Every human heart longs to experience the manifest presence of God. Augustine said that our hearts are restless until they find rest in Him. If you long for that rest, here's the equation:

Clean on the inside + compassion on the outside = God in the midst.

⑤ **Read Isaiah's full promise in the margin (Isa. 58:10-11). Underline the benefits. I've underlined one for you.**

All that we are will rise into the light of who God is and dispel the darkness that hangs over our world and too often over our own hearts. Gloom turns to brightness. God guides you and gives you strength. He quenches your thirst.

Some of you wonder, "Will anything ever grow in my life again?" If you've ever wondered not *when* but *if* your heart to worship can ever return, the answer is "yes, it can."

🍃 **Close today's study with a time of prayer and worship. Ask God what He wants you to do in response to today's lesson.**

> God's presence quickly stalls in a stingy heart.

> **Isaiah 58:10-11—** *"Then your light will rise in darkness And your gloom will become like midday. And the LORD will continually guide you, And satisfy your desire in scorched places, And give strength to your bones; And you will be like a watered garden, And like a spring of water whose waters do not fail."*

DAY FIVE *Responding to God in Worship*

Today's Walk in the Word
John 4:24—*"God is spirit, and those who worship Him must worship in spirit and truth."*

Meditate on God's Name
LORD God, compassionate and gracious, slow to anger, and abounding in lovingkindness and truth (Exodus 34:6)

Talk to the Lord
Lord God, I want to worship You in spirit and truth. Teach me to do that. I thank You for the model of compassion, grace, patience, lovingkindness, and truth You provide for me to follow. Guide me and enable me to live my life like that. In fact, I pray that You will be so evident in my life that others who meet me will come face to face with the Christ who lives in me. Let my light shine! Amen.

Write Your Memory Verse
Isaiah 58:2—

_____

_____

_____

_____

_____

🖋 **Read Today's Walk in the Word verse in the margin, meditate on God's name, and talk to the Lord in prayer as you begin.**

Has Isaiah 58 given you a renewed vision of what your life can be like with God in the center and on the throne? He may not be there right now, but He's waiting. For your worship of God to grip you with His greatness, you may have some hard work ahead of you. Take what you've learned from our study and bring it to God in humble submission. The wonder of getting lost in His worship and praise waits for you up ahead. Don't miss another day. "Great is the LORD and greatly to be praised" (Ps. 145:3, NKJV). Let that greatness grip you as never before.

① **In this chapter we talked about three reasons God would ignore our worship: we are being selfish, strife-filled, or surface-y. Do any of these apply to you? If so, review that reason on pages 102-105. Write on a separate paper what you need to do or quit doing to bring your life in line.**

② **If you are not experiencing freedom in Christ because of sin, confess it and turn to the Lord for strength to walk in victory.**

③ **To whom (hungry, homeless poor, naked and helpless, family) or in what way have you sensed God wants you to show His compassion? Write a name or people group below and describe what you think you need to do and when. Make it a deliberate choice to put His heart into action in your life. Ask a friend to keep you accountable to do it or, better yet, do it together.**

_____

_____

④ **Read the following six Scripture passages that each describe a different benefit we have as God's "children of light." On a separate paper, write out a principle for living that will encourage you to walk with God.**
Psalm 89:15   Psalm 119:105   Proverbs 4:18   1 John 1:7
Proverbs 6:20-23   Isaiah 2:5   Ephesians 5:7-10

③ Meditate on Isaiah 58:8-9. How has God's greatness been manifested in your life in any of these five categories? How has His greatness changed you in the last 12 hours? In the last week? Make a note of instances in the margin.

#1 Light. " 'Then your light will break out like the dawn' "
#2 Recovery. " 'And your recovery will speedily spring forth;' "
#3 Righteousness. " 'And your righteousness will go before you;' "
#4 Protection. " 'The glory of the Lord will be your rear guard.' "
#5 Presence. " 'Then you will call, and the LORD will answer;
   you will cry, and He will say, "Here I am." ' "

🍃 Reflect on the following questions that may help you prepare yourself for the kind of worship that God ignites. If you need to make some changes, write notes to yourself in the margin or on separate paper. Then begin to make those changes.

1. Are you selfish, self-centered, more concerned and focused on your own desires than God's desires?
2. Do you have broken relationships that have not been reconciled? Are you filled with strife and conflict?
3. Are you focused on externals, ritual, insignificant, or superficial things in worship rather than the Lord?
4. Are you clean on the inside and compassionate on the outside?

🍃 Close this week's study with a time of prayer. Pray slowly and personalize this prayer. Fill names in the blanks as you pray.

Oh Lord God, I open my heart to You and confess the places in my life that I have kept separate from my worship of You.
   I acknowledge that my attitude toward _____ has been wrong, and I ask Your forgiveness.
   I repent of my lack of compassion toward those in need (of my love, of my service, of my time, of my financial gifts.) I think especially of _____. Please help me as I strive to replace my stinginess with generosity.
   I confess that I have only thought of myself, especially in my relationship with _____. Help me be like Your Son, who became a servant. Give me opportunities to serve _____ and then the humility and courage to do it.
   I understand that You may be ignoring my worship right now because I have been trying to live the Christian life on my own terms. I repent of that right now, Lord, _____ (fill in date, time) and come to You on Your terms.
   With faith, I anticipate what You will do in my life in the coming hours, days, and weeks as I bow before You in sincere worship. I believe even now You are flooding my life with the reality of who You are. Thank you, Father. May Your greatness be lifted up before me and exalted in and through me. Amen.

Isaiah 58:8-9
"Then your light will break out like the dawn,
And your recovery will speedily spring forth;
And your righteousness will go before you;
The glory of the LORD will be your rear guard.
Then you will call, and the LORD will answer;
You will cry, and He will say, 'Here I am.' "

Week Seven

GRIPPED BY THE GREATNESS GOD OF

GRIPPED BY MY IDENTITY IN GOD

Follow the session plans in the leader's guide on page 142.

Discussion Guide on the Worship of God

1. What have you learned or experienced about the worship of God this week that has been most meaningful or life changing?
2. What are three reasons God ignores our worship? Which one do you believe is the most common reason people in your church may miss out on genuine worship and why? Which one is the greatest challenge for you and why?
3. How does a person come to experience freedom in Christ? Volunteers: Describe a time when you experienced or gained victory over a sin area in your life.
4. Describe a time when you expressed the compassion of Christ to a needy person. Tell what impact it had on you or others around you. If you responded to activity 3 on page 114, share your response and ask for prayer as you show God's compassion.
5. In same sex small groups share your needs for recovery and/or protection (pp. 111-112). Take time to pray for each need shared.
6. What are some of the benefits we have as "children of light"? (activity 4, p. 114)

DVD Message Notes on My Identity in God (21 minutes)
Proverbs 23:7 (KJV)—"As [a man] thinketh in his heart, so is he."
Mistakes the World Makes About Identity Thoughts
1. _____ It Up, Baby!
2. Make Your _____ in the World
3. Have a Perfect _____

Daniel 4:37—" 'He is able to humble those who walk in _____.' "

God's Character	My Identity	My Attitude
1. God is _____.	I am chosen.	I can have confidence.
2. God is present.	I am _____.	I can have perseverance.
3. God is loving.	I am valued.	I can have _____.
4. God is faithful.	I am heard.	I can have peace.
5. God is patient.	I am forgiven.	I can have praise.

Responding to the Message

1. How does our thinking affect our lives and character?
2. What are some of the ways you've observed people trying to achieve significance through an identity based on pseudo solutions?
3. How are identity thoughts and attitudes affected by God's character?
4. Which one of the three identity thoughts dealt with in the video is most meaningful to you and why?

Preview Statements for This Week's Study

- Until we can honestly affirm: "I am who God says I am, and that's all that matters," our lives will be restless indeed.
- Only in our Creator can we discover all we are and were made to become.
- God put you on His most wanted list. Let that reality grip you and shape your identity.
- I belong to God Almighty—the eternal One, and His love isn't going away.
- He hears the most stumbling or broken cry, the whisper, the sigh, and the requests we feel when we don't even know how to begin.
- Your true identity will be a strong foundation when the challenges of life come your way.

Snapshot Summary
To be gripped by God's greatness is to understand not only who He is but who you are because of Him.

My Goal for You
I want you to understand God's character and your identity in Him so that you will have healthy spiritual attitudes.

Key Verse to Memorize
Isaiah 43:1—*" 'Do not fear, for I have redeemed you; I have called you by name; you are Mine!' "*

This Week's Mountaintop in Isaiah—Isaiah 43:1-21 (Selected Verses)

[1] *Thus says the LORD, your Creator, O Jacob, and He who formed you, O Israel, "Do not fear, for I have redeemed you; I have called you by name; you are Mine!*
[2] *"When you pass through the waters, I will be with you; and through the rivers, they will not overflow you. When you walk through the fire, you will not be scorched, nor will the flame burn you.*
[3] *"For I am the LORD your God, the Holy One of Israel, your Savior; I have given Egypt as your ransom, Cush and Seba in your place.*
[4] *"Since you are precious in My sight, since you are honored and I love you, I will give other men in your place and other peoples in exchange for your life.*
[5] *"Do not fear, for I am with you; I will bring your offspring from the east, and gather you from the west.*
[10] *"You are My witnesses," declares the LORD, "And My servant whom I have chosen, so that you may know and believe Me and understand that I am He. Before Me there was no God formed, and there will be none after Me.*

It Happened to Me

For as long as I can remember I have had a deep and abiding fear about losing one of my children to death. As a pastor, I've stood too often with heart-broken parents at the head of tiny caskets and shared words of comfort I knew were not adequate. At least not then.

It was torture to see Luke, our oldest son, drive the family car away for the first time. As I lost control of 16 years of successful protection, I secretly feared if I lost a child I might somehow lose my faith too.

I got used to them being out on the road after a while but simmering under the surface was a certain something I couldn't put my finger on. Even when Landon, our second son, began to drive, my fear stayed focused on Luke.

In August 2004, Luke headed to Moody Bible Institute. It was hard to see him go. But he was thriving, and I was thrilled that we would meet up at our church camp for Labor Day weekend. He picked up a friend for the 250-mile trek to the Michigan campground. I was already in Grand Rapids for some ministry-related meetings. Suddenly, in the middle of an afternoon meeting, I had a strong prompting in my spirit to call Luke and was a little anxious not to reach him. *He's on the road and probably out of cellular range,* I thought.

When the meetings ended, I reached for my cell phone and tried, again unsuccessfully, to contact Luke. Moments later my message notification rang. The message was from Kathy. She asked me to call her immediately.

"Luke's been in an accident," she said. "But he's OK."

I fired off questions and she calmly gave me the number of a motorist who had seen the accident and stopped to help.

I quickly pulled over, took the number down, and dialed. Luke had apparently blown out a tire and lost control of the vehicle. The boy traveling with him was unhurt, but Luke had several cuts and both were taken to the hospital.

I met Kathy at the exit just up the freeway, and we rushed to the hospital to retrieve our son.

We were not prepared for our first sight of Luke in the hospital. His head and chest were covered with blood, and he was crying out from the pain. Examinations revealed a number of lacerations from where his head struck the pavement through the shattered driver side window. Glass was imbedded in his skull, but the doctor felt his recovery would be full.

Police concurred that the SUV had rolled over at least three times and landed right-side up in the ditch. The car had burst into flames in the engine region, but others had pulled Luke from the vehicle and put out the fire.

X-rays revealed nothing of concern in the neck region, and we were greatly relieved when the doctor announced Luke's release several hours later. However, when he tried to get up, the throbbing in his neck became excruciating. The doctor feared an injury the X-ray had not revealed and ordered an MRI.

Before the hour was out, the diagnosis was in: "three non-displaced fractures in C2, the second vertebrae below the skull."

"He broke his neck?" "Yes," the doctor said. Normally a trauma of this sort displaces the broken bones, causing paralysis or death. "He is very lucky to be alive," the doctor told us.

Luke would have to wear a halo device for 8 to 12 weeks and see a specialist in Chicago about further surgery. Kathy and I huddled in grateful prayer. We worshiped the Lord for mercy shown and undeserved.

By God's grace Luke was released for an ambulance ride to Chicago on Labor Day and within a week he was sleeping well and gaining strength. As the son of a radio preacher, he had hoped for some anonymity at Moody; but it was not to be. His halo made him a little hard to miss as he commuted to campus; and a supportive, praying student body continually encouraged him.

It was a very tough autumn. But the Lord gave Luke grace and was clearly shaping his character with a full-size chisel.

We all learned a lot—some of which is still too tender to talk about. I've mulled over how all the possible variations on the accident would have shaped a different outcome … and our son would be with the Lord. I have thought and prayed often, wondering if I would have passed the test of faithfulness had our Lord chosen to take our first son home. I know firsthand how essential it is that we base all of our identity in the Lord Himself. I know this because … it happened to me.

DAY 1 *A Faulty Identity*

🌿 Read Today's Walk in the Word verse in the margin, meditate on God's name, and talk to the Lord in prayer.

① **Does Isaiah 43:1 (Today's Walk in the Word) "wow" you the way it does me? I want you to memorize the last half of that verse this week. But if you want to memorize it all, be my guest! Begin memorizing it and fill in the blanks below.**

" 'Do not _____, for I have _____ you;

I have _____ you by _____; you are _____!' "

When we get to studying the mountaintop in Isaiah 43, you will have ample opportunity to be gripped by God's greatness as you realize who you are in God. But before we go there, I want us to take a look at some of the lame thinking people are doing about themselves.

WHAT ARE YOU THINKING?

"As [a man] thinks within himself, so is he" (Prov. 23:7, NASB). Your thoughts determine who you will become. For some of us that's a scary thought. Especially powerful are identity thoughts. These are thoughts not about where I am or what I am doing but about who I am.

Negative identity thoughts bring you down like, "Wow, I am such a loser. Won't I ever learn?" or "People only like me for a while. When they really get to know me, they always run away." But the problem is bigger than mere negativity. Some have identity thoughts that are way too positive. "Yes, you can count on me. I'm the man!" or "Forget my past performance, I'm still the best one for the job."

② **Write one positive or negative identity thought you have (or have had) about yourself.**

_____

③ **How would you evaluate your personal collection of identity thoughts about yourself? Check the one most like you.**
   ❏ a. I'm heavily weighted on the negative side. I don't think very positively about myself.
   ❏ b. Hey, I've got it together. What can I say?
   ❏ c. I've got a mixture of both positive and negative identity thoughts. Sometimes I'm up, and sometimes I'm down.

Today's Walk in the Word
Isaiah 43:1—*"But now, thus says the LORD, your Creator, O Jacob,*
and He who formed you, O Israel,
'Do not fear, for I have redeemed you;
I have called you by name; you are Mine!' "

Meditate on God's Name
The Maker of all (Jeremiah 10:16)

Talk to the Lord
My Maker, my Creator, You have made me. You know me better than I know myself. I want to get my thinking in line with the truth You know about me—the me You've made me to be. Could it be that You would call me by name and make me Your own? What a wonderful thought. Grip me by Your greatness this week. Amen.

> What we think about ourselves really is a big deal.

PSEUDO
fake, pretend, bogus

Attitudes are patterns of thinking formed over a long period of time, and they are very difficult to change. I often speak with people surprised by their actions. "How could I have done that?" "I never dreamed I could do something so awful." Often we fail to see that our identity thoughts entrench our attitudes and in the end dictate our very actions. What we think about ourselves really is a big deal.

Our fellow humans are far better at diagnosing the debilitating affects of harmful identity thoughts than they are at finding a solution. Consider these three pseudo solutions that the world teaches us to counter the negative affects of poor identity thoughts.

Pseudo Solution #1: Pump It Up, Baby!
Some recommend a personal inflation. They say you need to "psyche yourself up!" Look in the mirror and say, "Dude, you're the man!" or "Sister, you've got it going on!" Regardless of the wrong you may have done the previous day and setting aside the matters in which you clearly need to change, you are to look yourself square in the eye and say, "I am still awesome, and today's gonna be the best day of my life."

④ **Have you ever used this approach to improve your feelings about yourself?** ❑ Yes ❑ No

⑤ **Describe the "Pump It Up, Baby" solution in your own words.**

_____

This is a common approach for many. Books are written to help you do it well. The problem is you can only lie to yourself for so long. You might say, "I'm a great guy," but you know in your heart you're not. The Bible says "the heart is more deceitful than all else and is desperately sick" (Jer. 17:9). The constant friction between what you tell yourself and what you know to be true eventually brings you down.

Pseudo Solution #2: Make Your Mark
Some of us are far too realistic to pump it up—so we try to build it up instead. Through our efforts to accomplish something of significance, we hope to convince ourselves and others how important we are. In our heads we imagine, "I'll build a company [or a ministry] that will make a phenomenal impact on others. People will see my work and acknowledge my value!" Most of us have poured far too much energy down that bottomless pit. Fact is, none of us can diagram our lives, nor can we accomplish everything we desire or dream. And if we did, it still wouldn't satisfy our longing for true identity.

⑤ **What is a second faulty way to improving identity thoughts?**

_____

Pseudo Solution #3: That Family Feeling

Even those who escape the traps of ego inflation and personal notoriety may end up retreating down a dead-end street. Acknowledging the emptiness of personal accomplishment, they pursue instead the road of family pride. Pouring themselves into their marriage and kids, they hope to find at home what they lost on Wall Street. The problem here is that growing a family is not like making cookies. Even if you follow the biblical recipe, things may come out all wrong. No one can guarantee the obedience of another. If my identity is too tightly attached to my family "success," I am headed for heartbreak in a hurry.

⑥ **Describe one way you've seen people try to improve their own feelings of worth through a child, spouse, or family.**

_____

⑦ **Match each pseudo solution with its description.**

_____ 1. Pump it up, Baby   a. Do something significant that will gain fame and recognition.

_____ 2. Make your mark   b. Be significant because of the success of those closest to you.

_____ 3. Family feeling   c. Positive thinking is the key to believing the best about yourself.

Finding the Missing Piece

The flashing neon sign that hangs over all of this says, "Duh! You've left out God." In the end there is nothing we can do to generate a message about ourselves that will satisfy the longing in our hearts. None of the pseudo solutions will do. Until we can honestly affirm, "I am who God says I am, and that's all that matters," our lives will be restless indeed. Oh the freedom of saying and meaning, "I'm not who my parents say I am; I am not who my boss says I am; I am not who my spouse, or even my appearance says I am." But instead … "I am who God says I am."

⑧ **How desperately do you want to know that kind of freedom? Check the one that is closest to your desires.**
- ❑ a. I'm desperate! I'm sick and tired of bad thoughts and feelings.
- ❑ b. You've got my attention. I'm ready for some improvements.
- ❑ c. I'm hopeless. I don't know if you can do anything to help me.
- ❑ d. I've learned to get my identity from God. But a refresher course is always a good thing.

If you're tired of looking for your true identity in all the wrong places, you're ready for Isaiah 43. If you feel hopeless, help is on the way. If your need is refreshment, Isaiah will not let you down.

🍂 **Close today's study with a time of prayer. Confess to the Lord any of the identity thoughts about yourself that you realize are faulty, pseudo, inadequate, painful, or just plain sinful. Give Him permission to renew your mind this week.**

> Until we can honestly affirm, "I am who God says I am, and that's all that matters," our lives will be restless indeed.

DAY TWO *Get a Grip on Your Identity in God*

Today's Walk in the Word
Isaiah 48:17—*"Thus says the*
LORD, your Redeemer, the Holy
One of Israel,
'I am the LORD your God,
who teaches you to profit,
Who leads you in the way
you should go.' "

Meditate on God's Name
Redeemer
(Isaiah 41:14; 47:4; 54:8; 63:16)

Talk to the Lord
O my Redeemer, the Holy One.
Today I worship You for all your
greatness you are revealing to
me. You are awesome! Thank
you for making me Your own,
for teaching me, for guiding
me in the ways I should go. Oh,
how I need You. Teach me about
Yourself and reveal to me the
ways I'm related to You. Amen.

Review Your Memory Verse
Isaiah 43:1—" *'Do not fear,*
for I have redeemed you;
I have called you by name;
you are Mine!' "

🖋 **Read Today's Walk in the Word verse in the margin, meditate on God's name, and talk to the Lord in prayer.**

Who Am I, Really?

Everyone is searching for the answer to that question. As you learned yesterday, positive thinking, making a difference, or riding the success of others are lame attempts at feeling worthy. None of these can ever reveal more than a mere shadow of who we truly are.

In this final mountaintop, we'll look at how God's greatness affects the most secret place in our world—our true identity. Only in our Creator can we discover all we are and were made to become. We will see that our identity is based upon who God is and how He chooses to relate to us. These true and correct identity thoughts will produce healthy attitudes that lead to right actions. We will study five combinations of God's character, our identity, and the resulting attitude.

① **We will study all five sets, but if you could only study one combination below, which one would you choose? Circle it.**

God's Character	My Identity	My Attitude
1. God is personal.	I am chosen.	I can have confidence.
2. God is present.	I am strong.	I can have perseverance.
3. God is loving.	I am valued.	I can have security.
4. God is faithful.	I am heard.	I can have peace.
5. God is patient.	I am forgiven.	I can have praise.

Because your thinking can affect your attitudes, I want you to fix these truths firmly in your mind. As we study each set, I will be asking you to recall God's character, your identity, and your attitude that results. By the end of the week you should not only be able to fill in this chart, but you should be gripped by the truth of who your are in God.

God's Name

Each day I've asked you to meditate on a name of God. Each name tells us something about who God is, what He does, or what He is like. God's character and activity have a profound affect on our identity.

② **Review the names of God at the beginning of each day. Write your favorite name below. You may have a favorite we didn't name. If so, write it also.**

_____

Your Redeemer

Redeemer is one of Isaiah's favorite names for God. He used it more than any other biblical writer. God the Redeemer paid the ransom for our souls, doing for us what we could never do. We sold ourselves to be slaves of sin, and God bought us back—He redeemed us. He paid our ransom.

God weaves this ribbon of redemption or ransom throughout the entire Bible. The Old Testament points forward to redemption coming through Jesus Christ (see Isa. 53:5). The Gospels introduce us to the Lamb of God who takes away the sins of the world (see John 1:29). God's Spirit comforts us that our Redeemer lives and intercedes for us (Heb. 7:25). Revelation directs our faith to the future when every tongue will worship, "Worthy is the Lamb that was slain" (see Rev. 5:12). The ribbon of ransom woven through history ties our hearts to God's heart through the blood of His Son Jesus, our Redeemer. I pray you will be gripped this week by what your Redeemer has done for you.

③ **Read the three Scriptures in the margin. Underline the words that describe what your Redeemer has done for you.**

Let's begin our look at your true identity in God. Here's the first set.

I AM CHOSEN

God Is Personal

"But now, thus says the LORD, your Creator, O Jacob, and He who formed you, O Israel" (Isa. 43:1). I love that word *formed*. God may have spoken the universe into existence, but He *formed* us. Genesis 2:7 uses *formed* to describe the creative process of making man from the dust. In Jeremiah 18 God uses the imagery of a potter carefully shaping the clay in his hands to describe God's relationship with His people. I love the days in elementary school when my teacher would get out the pottery wheel. It was so cool to see things formed before your eyes. That is, except when the thing being formed is you—then it's a bit scary, isn't it?

Anticipating that response, God adds: "Do not fear." Before you can even express your heart, He speaks right to it. "I know you're afraid … don't be." In two short phrases God affirms His total, absolute commitment to you. The first is "for I have redeemed you." In order for God to have a relationship with you, He had to personally pay for it. And you're not cheap. God paid your ransom with the death of His Son, Jesus Christ.

God's second word of personal commitment is "I have called you by name" (v. 1). For the past few years I have struggled with the reality of not knowing all the names of people in our church. I used to know everyone. But somewhere between hundreds and thousands, I lost track. I remember praying about that. The Lord was like, "James—I know their names. It's not about you communicating your love and care to everyone. It's about you bringing people to Me!" Wow, that was both hard to hear and incredibly freeing.

REDEEMER
The Lamb of God, Jesus Christ

REDEEM
To pay the required price to buy back something or someone sold by the original owner

Isaiah 53:5— *"He was pierced through for our transgressions, He was crushed for our iniquities; The chastening for our well-being fell upon Him, And by His scourging we are healed."*

John 1:29— *" 'Behold, the Lamb of God who takes away the sin of the world!' "*

Hebrews 7:25— *"He is able also to save forever those who draw near to God through Him, since He always lives to make intercession for them."*

"You are Mine" (v. 1). In the massive sea of humanity, now billions of people, only a few can say God has called them by name. Only a fraction of the world's population has received these incredibly defining words direct from the Creator: "You are Mine." Jesus tells us, " 'Many are called, but few are chosen' " (Matt. 22:14). If you are among the few who have been chosen ... wow!

⑥ **Name God's character by filling in the blank.**

God is _____. I am chosen. I can have confidence.

I Am Chosen

With all due respect to blood relatives, there is something powerful about being chosen. If you were adopted into a family, you were chosen. Your parents looked around and said, "We want her." Or "We choose him." If you are married, then you also know the wonder of being chosen. Out of all the girls in your high school or college, from all the boys in your city or state, your spouse chose you to share his or her life and every experience that will ever come your way.

However, even these powerful bonds can't compare to the truth that God in His infinite grace chose to set His love upon you!

- "Because he has loved Me, ... I will set him securely on high, because he has known My name" (Ps. 91:14).
- "He chose us ... before the foundation of the world" (Eph. 1:4).

Somehow, before the world was made, God looked into the future and chose to set His love upon you.

⑦ **Name God's character and your identity by filling in the blanks.**

God is _____. I am _____. I can have confidence.

I Can Have Confidence

When you begin to let the truth that God personally chose you settle down into your heart, the result is confidence. Isaiah 43:1 says, "He who formed you, O Israel, 'Do not fear.' " The opposite of fear is confidence. When you're gripped by His personal interest in you, you can know with certainty that you are not who your resumé, your performance, your friends or enemies say you are. Instead you accept that you are who God says you are. For no good reason of your own, God put you on His most wanted list. Let that reality grip you and shape your identity.

⑧ **Fill in the blanks below for character, identity, and attitude.**

God is _____. I am _____. I can have _____.

✎ **Close your study today by telling the Lord how much you love being His. Thank Him for choosing you. Ask Him to firmly establish an attitude of confidence in your life.**

If you are among the few who have been chosen ... wow!

Ephesians 1:4
"He chose us in Him before the foundation of the world, that we would be holy and blameless before Him."

God put you on His most wanted list. Let that reality grip you and shape your identity.

DAY 3 *I Am Strong and Valued*

🌿 **Read Today's Walk in the Word verses in the margin, meditate on God's name, and talk to the Lord in prayer.**

① **Yesterday you learned that you are chosen. As a review, fill in the blanks for God's character and your attitude.**

God is _____. I am chosen. I can have _____.

I AM STRONG

God Is Present

A few years ago, a pop song topped the chart touting "God is watching us from a distance." But the song is wrong. God isn't looking at the earth like some astronaut from orbit. He doesn't need a telescope to see your need. God is right here with us. A name for the coming Christ—*Immanuel*—in Isaiah 7:14 means, "God with us" (Matt. 1:23).

Look at verse 2. "When you pass through the waters, I will be with you; and through the rivers, they will not overflow you. When you walk through the fire, you will not be scorched, nor will the flame burn you." Here's the truth about God. He is with you—especially in hardship. God specifically measures your trials. "The heat will be just enough to refine you; I have My hand on the thermostat," He says. "I'm watching. Trust Me!" It's the same picture in the flood. God says that when you pass through the waters, they will not overflow you. As we face tough times we wonder, *How deep will the water get? How long will I be able to touch bottom?* But God assures us, "I'm controlling the rising tide. I'm measuring the intensity of this trial." Both pictures shout loudly: God is "in the building" and very attentive.

② **Name God's character by filling in the blank.**

God is _____. I am strong. I can have perseverance.

I Am Strong

Why would a loving God allow this kind of hardship? Answer: to show us how strong we can be in Him. Deep within us is a sinful inclination toward independence. We think we can make it on our own, and we want to prove it is true. The world mocks and ridicules human weakness and celebrates those who shake their fist and proclaim, "I will survive." Fact is, we are all very weak.

Human strength is an illusion. God lovingly uses hardship and painful circumstances to teach us how badly we need Him. Like Paul

Today's Walk in the Word
Ephesians 1:3-4—*"Blessed be the God and Father of our Lord Jesus Christ, who has blessed us with every spiritual blessing in the heavenly places in Christ, just as He chose us in Him before the foundation of the world."*

Meditate on God's Name
He who formed you (Isaiah 43:1)

Talk to the Lord
My Creator and Lord, how unworthy I am to be redeemed by You. Yet, I am chosen, strong, valued, heard, and forgiven because of You. I want to know my identity in You so clearly that my life will be characterized by confidence, perseverance, security, peace, and praise. Transform my thinking. In Jesus' name. Amen.

Review Your Memory Verse
Isaiah 43:1—" 'Do not fear,
    for I have redeemed you;
I have called you by name;
    you are Mine!' "

said, "When I am weak, then I am strong" (2 Cor. 12:10). Only when God shows me how weak I am do I reach for Him like a drowning man. God is committed to making that moment possible for each of us. Then, when you are gripped by God's greatness in your life, you can echo the apostle Paul's victory cry, "I can do all things through Christ who strengthens me" (Phil. 4:13, NKJV). Only when we exchange our triple-A-battery strength for God's nuclear power do we fully realize the purpose of trials. In Him we are strong.

③ **Name God's character and your identity by filling in the blanks.**

God is _____. I am _____. I can have perseverance.

PERSEVERANCE
Persistent hard work, endurance, diligence, dedication

> Let your identity in God grip your heart, shape your thoughts, and dictate the destiny almighty God has ordained for you.

I Can Have Perseverance
The other day I was working on the computer with my oldest son, Luke. When he signed on, I asked him, "What's your password?" He said, "Keep on." That is a great password. He has no idea how critical those two words are to success in life. The biblical word is *endurance* or "staying power"—the ability to remain under the pressure. Nothing is more essential to success in the Christian life than that. Faith gets you started, but perseverance keeps you going.

Let me say boldly: You are not going to give up! God is present with you, He is giving you the strength you need and you are not going under—no way! You are an overcomer in a world of quitters. Let your identity in God grip your heart, shape your thoughts, and dictate the destiny almighty God has ordained for you. Keep on!

④ **Fill in the blanks below for character, identity, and attitude.**

God is _____. I am _____. I can have _____.

🌿 **Pray and ask God to help you believe the truth about your identity in Him, and ask Him to firmly establish an attitude of perseverance in your life.**

I AM VALUED

God Is Loving
Isaiah 43:3-4 will help us understand God's heart.

⑤ **Read Isaiah 43:3-4 in the margin and underline the words that describe God's thoughts about Israel.**

They are precious in God's sight, and He loves them. It sounds a bit alien at first, but stay with me. Where in the world are Cush and Seba? They are provinces in southern Egypt. Isaiah's original audience had slavery on their minds, so God references their ancient history. "Remember when I delivered you out of slavery?" The ransom for their freedom was the lives of the Egyptians.

Isaiah 43:3-4

" 'For I am the LORD your God,
The Holy One of Israel, your
    Savior;
I have given Egypt as your
    ransom,
Cush and Seba in your place.
Since you are precious in My
    sight,
Since you are honored and I
    love you,
I will give other men in your
    place and other peoples in
    exchange for your life.' "

"Remember all that bloodshed? The plagues and then the midnight deaths of the firstborn. Then as you fled, the Egyptian army drowned at the bottom of the Red Sea. Remember? It happened!" Here's the principle: God says, "I will deliver you even at the expense of others."

Look at the last three words in verse 3: " 'in your place.' " The same principle is at the end of verse 4: " 'I will give other men in your place and other peoples in exchange for your life.' " What a humbling, haunting truth.

This principle of substitution is all over the Scripture. Isaiah expands it in chapter 53: "All we like sheep have gone astray; we have turned, every one, to his own way; and the LORD has laid on Him [speaking of Christ prophetically] the iniquity of us all" (v. 6, NKJV). What the Old Testament pictures and promises the New Testament provides and proclaims. Second Corinthians 5:21 says, "He made Him who knew no sin to be sin on our behalf, so that we might become the righteousness of God in Him." When I think about all those Egyptians dying at the bottom of the Red Sea rather than the Israelites, it doesn't bother me that much. They were pagans who rejected God; they deserved punishment and in the end. It was war.

Jesus dying for you and me is another matter entirely. He was pure and spotless, righteous and holy. He deserved no judgment. He took judgment upon Himself as God's Son so that we might be forgiven. Amazing! As we learned in week 1, God's holiness demands that sin not be casually dismissed. In order to forgive us, someone had to pay the penalty for our sin.

But why would Jesus choose to do that? The answer is right here in verse 4, " 'Since you are precious in My sight, since you are honored and I love you.' " In the original Hebrew language, each of those phrases is in the perfect tense. It describes God's affection for us from eternity past to the present, and forever into the future.

"How could He? I've done some things that I can't even talk about." You're still not getting it. Let go of the things that have distorted your perspective of who you are. Erase from your mind all distorted perspectives your behavior and pride may have engraved upon your identity. Embrace the message almighty God is singing over you this moment, "You are precious in My sight … and I love you!"

⑥ **Name God's character by filling in the blank.**

God is _____. I am valued. I can have security.

I Am Valued

Does God love me because I'm valuable? No. That message is not in the Bible. There is nothing in us that makes us valuable. The fact that God values us says something about God. It says nothing about us. God did not set His love upon you because you have something going on that your next-door neighbor doesn't. We are not valuable in ourselves and—believe it or not—that is great news.

If God loves us because of something He sees in us, then what happens when we change? When we fail, or fall, or fade away? Will

> Embrace the message almighty God is singing over you this moment, "You are precious in My sight … and I love you!"

God's heart change? Maybe His love goes away. No! The distinction may seem minor but it's massive. We are not valuable, we are valued. Get the difference?

In 1996, Jacqueline Kennedy Onassis's estate was auctioned, and people went crazy. A worn footstool went for $33,350. A silver tape measure sold for $48,875. The night's highest price was for a walnut tobacco humidor that had belonged to President John Kennedy. That cigar box sold for $574,500! Here's the point: That stuff was valued not because of any intrinsic worth, but because of its owner. It's the same with us. We're the tarnished tobacco box, but we belong to God. My value is not based upon who *I* am but *whose* I am. I belong to God Almighty—the eternal One, and His love isn't going away.

⑦ **Name God's character and your identity by filling in the blanks.**

God is _____. I am _____. I can have security.

I Can Have Security

So, if I didn't earn His love; if I didn't pay for it; if I didn't deserve it, then get this—I'm not the one who has to keep it going. I am secure.

Fifty percent of marriages end in divorce. A career job is one that lasts more than five years before the company folds or fires you or finds a new technology to replace you. People change churches like they change their cars. And the idea "friends for life" seems to have gone the way of ice boxes and typewriters. With so much rejection swirling in the air, it's no wonder the matter of insecurity is epidemic. Everyone seems to be wondering when the hammer will fall and the pain of a broken relationship will be felt yet again.

Let's build our lives on the bedrock of a loving God who says we are valued by Him. That way, no matter how much change is crashing and burning around us, we can rest in the security of a loving God who says, "I am the LORD, I do not change" (Mal. 3:6, NKJV). He doesn't change whom He's chosen—the ones He loves. That's security!

⑧ **Fill in the blanks below for character, identity, and attitude.**

God is _____. I am _____. I can have _____.

🌿 **Pray and ask God to help you believe the truth about your identity in Him, and ask Him to firmly establish an attitude of security in your life.**

> I belong to God Almighty—the eternal One, and His love isn't going away.

DAY 4 *I Am Heard and Forgiven*

🖋 **Read Today's Walk in the Word verses in the margin, meditate on God's name, and talk to the Lord in prayer as you begin.**

I AM HEARD

God Is Faithful

Can't you feel the joy growing inside you right now? To think God has personally chosen me brings such confidence! Beyond that, God's presence gives me strength to persevere. God's love tells me I am valued and allows me to feel secure.

Wouldn't it be great if your family was all on that same page with you? Someone has said that parents are seldom happier than their most miserable child. I hope that's not true, but I do know that people have a hard time experiencing joy as long as someone in their family is hurting. No surprise then that right in the middle of Isaiah 43, God makes this incredible promise.

> "Do not fear, for I am with you; I will bring your offspring from the east, and gather you from the west. I will say to the north, 'Give them up!' And to the south, 'Do not hold them back.' Bring My sons from afar and My daughters from the ends of the earth, everyone who is called by My name, and whom I have created for My glory, whom I have formed, even whom I have made" (vv. 5-6).

As a pastor of a large church, I've prayed with more parents on behalf of more rebellious kids than I can count. Let me tell you one story to build your confidence in God's faithfulness.

The first time I met Emily, she was a seriously messed up 17 year old. She and her friends were headed in a bad direction fast. Though her parents pleaded with her to turn her life around, she seemed bent on her own destruction. The moment she finished high school she was out the door as fast as her feet could carry her. With a pair of extra shoes and the clothes on her back, she walked away from God and her parents and moved to the far side of the world. She ended up in Sipan, a tiny island in southeast Asia.

Her parents were brokenhearted. "Where is Emily tonight?" "What is she doing?" "Will we ever see her again?" They longed to know that their daughter was even alive. One, two, five years went by—I remember a lot of prayer meetings when we called out to God for Emily. But honestly, it all seemed so hopeless.

In Sipan, Emily got involved with a man named Kojo. He was wealthy, seductive, and lavished on her everything she thought she

Today's Walk in the Word
Psalm 116:1-2, ESV— *"I love the LORD, because he has heard my voice and my pleas for mercy. Because he inclined his ear to me, therefore I will call on him as long as I live."*

Meditate on God's Names
Faithful and True
(Revelation 19:11)
The LORD your Redeemer
(Isaiah 43:14)

Talk to the Lord
Faithful and True God, I thank You that even in Your vastness and greatness You choose to hear my prayers. I thank You that I can trust You to remain faithful, even when I fail. I'm learning much about myself that is wonderful because of You. Continue to open my eyes to see and my mind to understand my identity in You. Amen.

Review Your Memory Verse
Isaiah 43:1—" *'Do not fear, for I have redeemed you; I have called you by name; you are Mine!' "*

wanted. Together they had a daughter. But Emily couldn't find the peace she craved. She said, "I would walk up and down the beach with my little girl looking for shells and beautiful things. From a human perspective I had everything, but inside I was empty."

All this time her parents were persisting in prayer and asking God to bring home their daughter. Was God listening to those prayers? Many days the answer appeared to be a resounding no.

But then Emily's world collapsed. There was trouble with Kojo. She found out he was a member of the Akusa, the Japanese Mafia. At one point he was thrown into jail, but quickly posted a million dollars cash bond to get out. She realized she had to get away, yet that tiny island became like a prison. She was terrified.

Late one night Kojo said he was coming over. Emily, fearing a confrontation, watched from above as he got out of his car. In that moment men poured out of the jungle around his car and violently grabbed him. The police were breaking up Kojo's drug ring.

Later we learned that at the very moment this was going on her parents were praying in Chicago—praying for God to get hold of their daughter and bring her safely home. In the confusion of Kojo's arrest, Emily escaped to Guam and immediately called her parents. Crying and uncertain of their response, she dialed home and heard her mother say, "Emily, we love you. Come home." As soon as she could, she jumped on a plane and flew back to Chicago.

In a recent worship service, I noticed Emily as I was preaching and rejoiced in the obvious transformation God had brought to her life. Her whole appearance had changed. The anger and rebellion were gone, replaced by a joy that only comes through obedience to the Lord. As I saw her I thought of Isaiah 43 and the promise God makes about bringing our family home no matter how far gone they appear to be. It's a promise you can bank on and use to increase your faith.

① **Name God's character by filling in the blank.**

God is _____. I am heard. I can have peace.

I Am Heard

Even when you don't feel it or see it, God hears you! He doesn't always answer how or when you want, but God does answer prayer. It's not about you saying the right words or following any silly formula. He doesn't give preference to the eloquent or to the most persuasive. He hears the most stumbling or broken cry, the whisper, the sigh, and the requests we feel when we don't even know how to begin. The psalmist writes, "I love the LORD, because he has heard my voice and my pleas for mercy. Because he inclined his ear to me, therefore I will call on him as long as I live" (Ps. 116:1-2, ESV).

Maybe you too have a prodigal, a child who wants nothing to do with God, and you're praying for him or her to return. Maybe you're praying for wisdom, protection, or for a future spouse for a child. Are you calling out for the conversion of an adult child? Keep on praying. God hears you, and He's working in ways beyond your imagination.

> He hears the most stumbling or broken cry, the whisper, the sigh, and the requests we feel when we don't even know how to begin.

② **Name God's character and your identity by filling in the blanks.**

God is _____. I am _____. I can have peace.

I Can Have Peace

God is faithful; you are heard. Result? You have the choice to follow His program and claim His peace.

③ **Read the promise in Philippians 4:6-7 in the margin and underline what God gives to guard your heart and mind.**

Get it? Worry about nothing. Pray about everything. Expect God's *peace* to stand guard around your mind and heart. Why? Because He isn't fickle about keeping His promises. If your heart is a storm, let God hear from you. Let His faithfulness grip your heart with peace.

④ **Fill in the blanks below for character, identity, and attitude.**

God is _____. I am _____. I can have _____.

🌿 **Pray and ask God to help you believe the truth about your identity in Him, and ask Him to firmly establish an attitude of peace in your life. Take your persistent requests to Him.**

Philippians 4:6-7—"*Be anxious for nothing, but in everything by prayer and supplication with thanksgiving let your requests be made known to God. And the peace of God, which surpasses all comprehension, shall guard your hearts and your minds in Christ Jesus.*"

I AM FORGIVEN

God Is Patient

" 'Do not call to mind the former things, or ponder things of the past' " (Isa. 43:18). Amazing, isn't it? Voices for personal growth and well-being in our world almost unanimously call for us to dig up our past in order to do better in the future. God says, "Do not." Being gripped by God's greatness is all about today and tomorrow, not yesterday.

God is patient with you. He's not keeping tabs on how many times you fall into a certain sin. Do you think what you've done shocks Him? Early in the chapter God identified Himself as the One who formed you (Isa. 43:1). He knows what you're about. Beyond that, God is prompting you to forgive and release those who have injured you so you can go forward into deeper experiences with Him. He's all about doing a new work in you today! Look at similar messages in Isaiah and Philippians:

" 'Do not call to mind the former things, or ponder things of the past. Behold, I will do something new, now it will spring forth' " (Isa. 43:18-19).

"Forgetting those things which are behind … reaching forward to those things which are ahead" (Phil. 3:13, NKJV).

Put the pain and disappointment of past failures behind you and press yourself hard in the grip of this incredibly patient God.

④ **Name God's character by filling in the blank.**

God is _____. I am forgiven. I can have praise.

Being gripped by God's greatness is all about today and tomorrow, not yesterday.

Truths About God's Forgiveness

1. It is God's nature to forgive. "For You, Lord, are good, and ready to forgive, and abundant in mercy to all those who call upon You" (Psalm 86:5, NKJV).

2. There is no limit to God's forgiveness. " 'If [your brother] sins against you seven times a day, and returns to you seven times, saying, "I repent," forgive him' " (Luke 17:4).

3. Forgiveness was in our Lord's heart as He died on the cross. "But Jesus was saying 'Father, forgive them' " (Luke 23:34).

4. God forgives us only because Christ died to pay for our sins. "In [Christ] we have redemption through His blood, the forgiveness of sins" (Ephesians 1:7, NKJV).

5. God is always ready to forgive us. "If we confess our sins, He is faithful and just to forgive us" (1 John 1:9, NKJV).

PRAISE
Giving honor, ascribing worth

I Am Forgiven

The only reason you can forgive is because you have been forgiven. Wanna get blessed? Do what I did and read every verse in the Bible that describes God's forgiveness. In case you don't get to it soon, here are the highlights:

⑤ **Read the truths about God's forgiveness in the margin.**

⑥ **Name God's character and your identity by filling in the blanks.**

God is _____. I am _____. I can have praise.

I Can Have Praise

Every heart that truly comprehends the reality of God's forgiveness bursts forth in a fountain of praise that drenches everyone in the near vicinity. "The beasts of the field will glorify Me; the jackals and the ostriches; because I have given waters in the wilderness and rivers in the desert, to give drink to My chosen people. The people whom I formed for Myself, will declare My praise" (vv. 20-21).

"I really like your hat" is not praise. Praise is more than a compliment. Praise is giving honor; it's ascribing worth to a superior. When we praise God, we express joy in His very nature and thank Him for His goodness.

When are we to praise? Right now. And at all times. We are called to bless the Lord when we see His goodness and when we don't. We are commanded to praise God in both of those circumstances.

To really be gripped by your identity in God's greatness, you must wade out of the shallow waters of self-absorption into the deep waters of praising Him at all times for all things. Remember, God formed you for that very purpose. Embrace your identity as a forgiven worshiper of this all-patient God. This moment He invites you to move more deeply into who He created you to be.

⑦ **Fill in the blanks below for character, identity, and attitude.**

God is _____. I am _____. I can have _____.

🌿 **Pray and ask God to help you believe the truth about your identity in Him, and ask Him to firmly establish an attitude of praise in your life.**

🌿 **Close today's study by bringing to the Lord in prayer your deepest burden for yourself or someone close to you. Thank Him for being One who hears prayer.**

DAY 5 *Living in My God-Given Identity*

🍃 **Read Today's Walk in the Word verses in the margin, meditate on God's name, and talk to the Lord in prayer as you begin today's study.**

Let's review what you've learned about your identity in God.

① **Use words from the following list to complete the chart. You may miss arranging items in the same order (1-5) but try to get the right combinations. When you finish, check your work. If you need help see page 122.**

chosen   confidence   faithful
forgiven   heard   loving
patient   peace   perseverance
personal   praise   present
security   strong   valued

God's Character	My Identity	My Attitude
1. God is _____.	I am _____.	I can have _____.
2. God is _____.	I am _____.	I can have _____.
3. God is _____.	I am _____.	I can have _____.
4. God is _____.	I am _____.	I can have _____.
5. God is _____.	I am _____.	I can have _____.

You can either base your identity in the faulty sources, or you can find your true identity in God. An identity built on faulty sources will let you down in a crisis. Your true identity will be a strong foundation when the challenges of life come your way.

② **Which of the following provides a solid and lasting foundation for your life? Check one.**
❑ a. My identity based upon my relationship with God
❑ b. My identity based upon my accomplishments
❑ c. My identity based upon my family members
❑ d. My identity based upon the positive thoughts I think

You've got it! Your only solid and lasting foundation for life is found in your relationship with God. Remember my story about Luke's

Today's Walk in the Word
Psalm 145:3-7— *"Great is the LORD, and highly to be praised; And His greatness is unsearchable. One generation shall praise Your works to another, And shall declare Your mighty acts. On the glorious splendor of Your majesty, And on Your wonderful works, I will meditate. Men shall speak of the power of Your awesome acts; And I will tell of Your greatness. They shall eagerly utter the memory of Your abundant goodness, And shall shout joyfully of Your righteousness.*

Meditate on God's Name
Great and Awesome God
(Deuteronomy 7:21)

Talk to the Lord
Great God, words are inadequate to express Your greatness. But, like the psalmist, I want to declare to the next generation
• your mighty acts;
• your unsearchable greatness;
• your glorious splendor;
• your majesty;
• your wonderful works;
• your power;
• your awesome acts;
• your abundant goodness;
• your righteousness;
• your greatness.
I praise You and worship Your holy name. Amen.

> When your identity is based upon your relationship with God, it doesn't change with circumstances.

accident at the beginning of the week (p. 118)? When something like that comes your way, you don't have time to get your identity straightened out. If you've built your identity around a child or some other person, your career, your popularity, or successes in life you are living on fragile territory. Those can be taken away or can collapse in a moment. But when your identity is based upon your relationship with God, it doesn't change with circumstances.

③ **Which of the following is true about you today? Check one.**
- ❑ a. My life is fragile, because I've based my identity on things that don't last forever.
- ❑ b. My life is secure, because my identity is based upon my everlasting relationship with God.

Search your life for any point of identity not rooted in God Himself. Make very sure God reigns supreme over this matter of your identity. Then if, in His sovereignty, He allows a profound loss to penetrate your world, you will not have to race to this place but will, in fact, have the strength of already being there. May God protect us from so loving our children (or our ministries, or our careers, or our spouses) that they become our identity and not our relationship with Him.

My prayer is, *Lord, allow us to love without adoring. Teach us to be involved with our loved ones but never idolize them. Teach us ever more deeply what it means to find our identity in You and in You to "live, and move, and have our being" (Acts 17:28, KJV).*

Don't Listen to the Enemy

It is a powerful thing to walk through this life with a firm confidence in your identity … as God knows you. But I want to alert you to our enemy, Satan, who is trying to mess you up about who you really are. If he can confuse you, he can accomplish a lot in your life.

If you've not committed your life to Jesus Christ, I need to talk very candidly. Satan is telling you you're OK just as you are. "You don't need Jesus. You're a good person—God should accept you into heaven just as you are. You're ready to meet God." That is a lie—you are not ready to meet God. If you die today, you will stand before a righteous, holy God and He will say, " 'I never knew you' " (Matt. 7:23).

You are not ready to meet God unless you have submitted your life to Jesus Christ. Please, get this matter settled today.

If you know Christ, Satan invests a lot of energy trying to get you to live apart from who you really are. He wants you to remember your failures. He wants to tuck those things in your pocket so he can throw them up in your face every time you try to take a step forward with God. He says, "You're a loser. You flunked out big time. God's not very fired up about you anymore." Everything Satan says to you is bent on your defeat and your ineffectiveness as a representative of Christ. He hates you because he hates Jesus Christ. Instead of letting those mental cancers grow, go back to what God says about you. Rehearse the list of the five things we talked about this week and how they define who you are and how you should live.

④ Photocopy or rewrite the grid on page 122 and put it somewhere you'll see it through the day. Instead of pumping yourself up with cotton candy phrases, return to what God's Word says.

⑤ Read and meditate on these additional truths from God's Word about your identity in Him. As you read, spend time thanking God for what He has done in your life.

1. **God's Word:** *"You have been bought with a price: therefore glorify God in your body"* (1 Cor. 6:20).
   My Identity: I have been bought with a price. I belong to Almighty God. I can glorify Him.

2. **God's Word:** *"He predestined us to adoption as sons through Jesus Christ to Himself, according to the kind intention of His will"* (Eph. 1:5).
   My Identity: I have been adopted as God's child. I'm His.

3. **God's Word:** *"When you were dead in your transgressions and the uncircumcision of your flesh, He made you alive together with Him, having forgiven us all our transgressions"* (Col. 2:13).
   My Identity: I have been redeemed and forgiven of all my sin.

4. **God's Word:** *"There is now no condemnation for those who are in Christ Jesus"* (Rom. 8:1).
   My Identity: I am no longer condemned, because I am in Christ.

5. **God's Word:** *"God causes all things to work together for good to those who love God, to those who are called according to His purpose"* (Rom. 8:28).
   My Identity: God works all things together for my good.

6. **God's Word:** *"I am convinced that neither death, nor life, nor angels, nor principalities, nor things present, nor things to come, nor powers, nor height, nor depth, nor any other created thing, will be able to separate us from the love of God, which is in Christ Jesus our Lord"* (Rom. 8:38-39).
   My Identity: I am loved. I cannot be separated from the love of God.

7. **God's Word:** *"Our citizenship is in heaven, from which also we eagerly wait for a Savior, the Lord Jesus Christ"* (Phil. 3:20).
   My Identity: I am a citizen of heaven.

8. **God's Word:** *" 'You are the salt of the earth. ... You are the light of the world. ' "* (Matt. 5:13-14).
   My Identity: I am the salt of the earth and the light of the world.

9. **God's Word:** *"Do you not know that you are a temple of God and that the Spirit of God dwells in you?"* (1 Cor. 3:16).
   My Identity: I am God's temple.

Write Your Memory Verse
Isaiah 43:1—

_____

_____

_____

_____

10. **God's Word:** *"We are His workmanship, created in Christ Jesus for good works, which God prepared beforehand so that we would walk in them" (Eph. 2:10).*
My Identity: I am God's workmanship—His masterpiece.

🌿 **Thank God right now for the realities revealed this week about your true identity. Ask Him to root them deep into your heart and prevent the enemy of your soul from stealing this seed of truth from you. Praise God for His faithfulness to you in all times and in all places. Close this study on your identity in God with the following prayer. Pray it slowly and thoughtfully. Personalize it. Make it your own.**

> Lord, thank You for the freedom I find in the truth of Your Word. I acknowledge before You in this moment of honesty that too often I have taken my identity from my successes, my relationships, or my performance. Lord, how ridiculous. Please forgive me.
>
> Let my only source of truth of who I am in You. Thank You for who You are. The truth about You eclipses everything. Thank You for Your love and Your faithfulness. Thank You for being personally present in my life. Help me live in light of that truth every day as I lift my voice to You in praise and in gratitude for Your amazing love.
>
> You are my Rock and my Redeemer, and I rest in You. Amen.

⑥ **Final review. Look back or think back through what you have studied about God's greatness in this book. Make notes in the margin about specific ways you have been gripped by God's greatness. Briefly describe below the most meaningful way you have been gripped by God's greatness during this study.**

_____

_____

_____

Week 1: Introduction to
      God's Greatness
Week 2: Holiness
Week 3: Awesomeness
Week 4: Sovereignty
Week 5: Works
Week 6: Worship
Week 7: Identity

⑦ **Which week's study has been most meaningful to you and why? For a reminder, the topics are listed in the margin.**

_____

_____

_____

_____

LEADER GUIDE

The following pages will give you information to help you prepare for and conduct eight small-group sessions for your study of *Gripped by the Greatness of God*.

Your Role as Small-Group Leader

You do not have to be a content expert to lead this Bible study. Your role is more that of a facilitator. James MacDonald will provide inspiring messages from God's Word each week in a DVD segment. During the week, participants will study this workbook and complete the interactive learning activities and prayer experiences. By use of these content segments and learning experiences, participants will be primed and ready to discuss the messages and share personal insights and experiences.

The two-page spread at the beginning of each week's lessons (one page for week one) provides a practical guide for your small-group session. On those pages you will find:

• a discussion guide for the previous week's study;
• DVD message notes for the teaching segment by James MacDonald;
• suggestions to guide discussion and sharing in response to the DVD message; and
• preview information for the upcoming study.

You will close each session with a final DVD testimony—It Happened to Me—by James MacDonald and then take time to pray for each other. In many cases those segments, together with times to pray, will fill your small-group session. If you have more time, you may choose to use some of the additional suggestions on the pages that follow. By using these resources, you can be a lead learner along with the other group participants. You could even share leadership if desired or necessary.

Pray

Because this is a spiritual process where God is involved, you need to pray for His leadership and involvement. Pray for wisdom. Pray that God will draw participants into the study for their benefit and His renown. Pray that God will genuinely grip you and your group members in such a way that you will be done with apathy. Pray that God's glory will be revealed as He works in your lives.

Set Time and Place for Small-Group Sessions

The small-group sessions can take place any time that is convenient for participants. Sundays, weekdays, or Saturdays will work. Daytime or evening. We recommend 90-minute sessions so you will have adequate time to view the DVD segments (25-33 minutes each week) and process what God has taught and done during the week. You could try shorter sessions, but you likely will find yourself pressed for time for members to adequately process what they are learning. You could conceivably study these messages without the DVD segments by just using the workbook. But once you've heard James MacDonald preach, you will not choose that option. Plan for plenty of time for members to be gripped by God's greatness as they study and pray together.

Groups may meet at the church building, in homes or apartments, in a community meeting room, in a workplace before or after work (or over lunch), in a school, or almost anyplace. The availability of a television and DVD player, sufficient space, and enough privacy to prevent interruption are the primary factors that may limit your choice of locations. Consider non-traditional places so members can use this as an outreach opportunity.

Determine Fees, If Any

Each participant will need a member book for the small-group study. Determine the cost for the participants so you can mention the cost in advertising the course. Usually people will be more faithful to use the member book and attend the sessions when they have made a personal investment in the resource. Be prepared to provide partial or complete scholarships where needed so no one will be prohibited from the study because of financial considerations.

Open or Closed Groups?

Decide whether your groups will be open or closed. An open group adds members at sessions after the first. A closed group does not add new members after the first or second session. You can choose either type group and have good experiences. New members will benefit, however, if they can study the content of the week's study prior to the session they join. But this is not absolutely necessary.

Group Size

The very best small-group dynamics will take place in groups of 8 to 15 members that remain consistent over time (in this case 8 sessions). Smaller groups may be too intimate for some. If members know and trust each other, smaller groups will be satisfactory. Larger groups are too big to allow everyone to participate. If you are really serious about enabling people to be gripped by God's greatness in the midst of His people, you don't want to have spectators. If you have more than 15, consider dividing into multiple groups.

If your church has multiple groups meeting at the same time at church, you may choose to watch the DVD messages as a large group and divide into small groups for content discussion and responding to the DVD message segments. If you use this format, keep people in the same small group each week. Don't require people to get acquainted and develop new relationships each week. They need to develop trust for sharing deeper thoughts and feelings as the study progresses.

Enlist Participants

Use your church's normal channels to advertise this study: bulletins, posters, newsletters, PowerPoint® slides before the service, announcements, church Web site, and so forth. The leader kit DVDs include a promotional segment (1 min. 14 sec.) that will introduce your folks to James MacDonald and invite their participation.

We assume that most participants will already have a saving relationship with Jesus Christ. However, you need not limit the group to believers only. Those who are yet to believe need to be introduced to our great God also. This might be the opportunity where they will encounter the living God and choose to trust Christ. In several places James extends an invitation for people to do so.

Order Resources

Each participant will need a member book (item 001288990). Because each person will need to give individual responses to the learning activities, a married couple will need to have two workbooks instead of sharing one copy. You will also need one leader kit (item 001288992) for your small group. The kit includes one copy of this member book and two DVDs with weekly teaching segments and testimonies plus a promotional segment.

Order copies by writing to LifeWay Church Resources Customer Service; One LifeWay Plaza; Nashville, TN 37234-0113; faxing (615) 251-5933; phoning (800) 458-2772; e-mailing *orderentry@ lifeway.com;* ordering online at *www.lifeway.com;* or visiting a LifeWay Christian Store.

Secure Equipment and Supplies

In addition to the member books and the leader kit, secure the following equipment and supplies for use during the sessions.

❑ television and DVD player
❑ name tags and markers
❑ marker board or chart paper and markers
❑ extra pens or pencils
❑ roster for keeping attendance records if desired
❑ index cards for member contact information

Preview Member Book and DVD Messages

If you prefer, study the entire member book and view all the DVD messages before beginning the study with your small group. You may, however, study one week ahead of your group and have a good experience. Before the first session, study week 1 (pp. 5-11) and view session 1 on the DVD. Be prepared to explain the way members will use this book to complete five daily lessons each week.

Prepare to Introduce James MacDonald

Read "About the Author" on page 4 and be prepared to introduce James to your group at the first session. If you would like to find out more about his ministries you can go to the Internet at:

• *www.harvestbible.org*
• *www.walkintheword.com*
• *www.lifeway.com/jamesmacdonald*

The latter site describes products and events by James MacDonald available from LifeWay.

Session Plans

In the following plans you will find suggestions for preparations to make before the session. Sessions 2-7 are divided into two relatively equal parts:

• Part 1—Discussion of the previous week's lessons
• Part 2—Viewing and discussing DVD segments

If you have a 90-minute session, each part should take about 45 minutes. If you have more or less time, adjust the times accordingly. If you only have one hour, use 20 minutes for part 1 and 40 minutes for part 2.

GROUP SESSION 1

This first session is your introductory session to this study of *Gripped by the Greatness of God*. During this session, participants will be introduced to the study by a DVD segment from James MacDonald. They will get acquainted with other members of the small-group, receive their member books, and preview the first week's lessons.

Before the Session

1. Set up the room so members can viewing the DVD segment. But keep it flexible enough so members can move around to face each other for discussion and sharing times.
2. Check the television and DVD player to make sure they are working and adjust the volume.
3. On a marker board or chart paper, write a list of the information you want to collect from each member: Name, mailing address, e-mail address, phone numbers, etc.
4. Provide name tags, markers, index cards, and pencils/pens.
5. Prepare a roster of people who have registered for the class. If they have not preregistered, be prepared to complete the roster as participants arrive.
6. Provide member books and arrange for the way you will collect fees for the books.

During the Session

1. As members arrive, greet them, ask them to prepare a name tag, and ask them to write the member information you desire on an index card.
2. Write their names on the roster or check them off as they receive and pay for their books.
3. Invite members to introduce themselves by sharing their names, an interesting fact about themselves that most people wouldn't know, and briefly why they decided to join this study group.
4. Invite members to turn to page 5. Direct them to the DVD Message Notes and explain that the notes summarize key points in the introductory segment from James MacDonald.
5. Introduce James MacDonald using information from page 4.
6. View the DVD Group Session 1 (27:55).
7. Ask members to get into smaller groups of 4 to 6 and discuss the three questions under Responding to the Message on page 5.

8. Back in the larger group, explain how members will use this member book to study five daily lessons each week.
9. Explain that each week James will share a testimony describing the way he has been gripped by God's greatness.
10. View the DVD segment It Happened to Me Session 1 (2:33).
11. Close the session in prayer that God will use this study to grip each member with His greatness.

GROUP SESSION 2

Before the Session

Set up the room, check your television/DVD player to make sure they are working properly, review the following session plans and determine which additional questions or activities would be most helpful to your group if time permits you to use them.

During the Session Part I (45 minutes)

1. Open the session with prayer or invite a volunteer to pray.
2. Ask members to turn to page 12 and follow the Discussion Guide to process what they have studied this week about God's holiness.

   As time allows, use questions or activities from the following list to continue processing the lessons studied this past week.
3. Share your responses to the following activities:
   - Recite Psalm 48:1 from memory (activity 1, p. 6)
   - Reasons in activities 1 and 2, p. 9.
   - Reasons in activities 1 and 2, p. 10.
   - Reasons in activities 1 and 2, p. 11
4. Review the following content:
   - What are three ways being gripped by God's greatness will impact our lives? (p. 8)
   - Why should we take the time to memorize Scriptures? (p. 10)
5. Discuss the following questions:
   - What are some tips you could give to others that help you memorize Scripture?
   - What Scripture, thought, or idea was most meaningful or significant to you this week?
   - Of all the topics you previewed this week, which one are you most interested in studying and why?

6. Pray for your group members that God will indeed grip them with His greatness. Ask God to begin to reveal Himself during the upcoming teaching on God's holiness.

During the Session Part 2 (45 minutes)
1. Point members to the DVD Message Notes on page 12 and view DVD Group Session 2 (20:34).
2. Guide the group to follow the instructions under Responding to the Message (pp. 12-13).
3. View DVD segment It Happened to Me Session 2 (2:59).
4. Invite a volunteer to pray for your group to be gripped by God's holiness this next week.

GROUP SESSION 3
Before the Session
Set up the room, check your television/DVD player to make sure they are working properly, review the following session plans and determine which additional questions or activities would be most helpful to your group if time permits you to use them.

During the Session Part I (45 minutes)
1. Open the session with prayer or invite a volunteer to pray.
2. Ask members to turn to page 34 and follow the Discussion Guide to process what they have studied this week. Make sure you allow plenty of time for sharing and prayer before considering other questions or activities below.

   As time allows, use questions or activities from the following list to continue processing the lessons studied this past week.
3. Share your responses to the following activities:
   • Recite Isaiah 6:3 from memory (activity 1, p. 15).
   • Activity 2, p. 15
   • Activity 2, p. 21
   • Activity 8, p. 25
   • Activity 6, p. 29
4. Review the following content:
   • How would you define holiness? (p. 15)
   • What is the essence of God's character? (p. 18)
5. Discuss the following questions:
   • Why do you think Isaiah was so fearful when He saw God's holiness?
   • What one thing do you sense God most wants you to do in response to this week's study and why?

6. Pray briefly that God will speak during the DVD teaching segment.

During the Session Part 2 (45 minutes)
1. Point members to the DVD Message Notes on page 34 and view the DVD Group Session 3 (20:41).
2. Guide the group to follow the instructions under Responding to the Message (p. 35).
3. View DVD segment It Happened to Me Session 3 (6:41).
4. Invite a volunteer to pray for your group to be gripped by God's awesomeness this next week.

GROUP SESSION 4
Before the Session
Set up the room, check your television/DVD player to make sure they are working properly, review the following session plans and determine which additional questions or activities would be most helpful to your group if time permits you to use them.

During the Session Part I (45 minutes)
1. Open the session with prayer or invite a volunteer to pray.
2. Ask members to turn to page 54 and follow the Discussion Guide to process what they have studied this week.

   As time allows use questions or activities from the following list to continue processing the lessons studied this past week.
3. Share your responses to the following activities:
   • Recite Deuteronomy 10:17 from memory (activity 1, p. 37).
   • Activity 2, p. 40
   • Activities 3 and 4, p. 42
   • Activity 7, p. 43
4. Review the following content:
   • How would you define *awesome*? (activity 3, p. 38)
   • What are some ways God has revealed His awesomeness?
5. Invite members to pray sentence prayers praising God for His awesomeness. Close by asking God to speak during the upcoming DVD message on God's sovereignty.

140 · GRIPPED BY THE GREATNESS OF GOD

During the Session Part 2 (45 minutes)

1. Point members to the DVD Message Notes on page 54 and view DVD Group Session 4 (20:15).
2. Guide the group to follow the instructions under Responding to the Message (p. 55).
3. View the DVD segment It Happened to Me Session 4 (12:06).
4. Invite a volunteer to pray for your group to be gripped by God's sovereignty this next week.

GROUP SESSION 5

Before the Session

Set up the room, check your television/DVD player to make sure they are working properly, review the following session plans and determine which additional questions or activities would be most helpful to your group if time permits you to use them.

During the Session Part I (45 minutes)

1. Open the session with prayer or invite a volunteer to pray.
2. Ask members to turn to page 76 and follow the Discussion Guide to process what they have studied this week.

    As time allows use questions or activities from the following list to continue processing the lessons studied this past week.
3. Share your responses to the following activities:
    • Recite Romans 8:28 from memory (activity 1, p. 57).
    • Activity 2, page 57
4. Discuss the following questions:
    • Which illustration of sovereignty was most helpful to you: the ocean liner or the chess master and why? (p. 67)
    • Volunteers, share a time when you experienced the struggle of submitting to God's sovereignty in a time of obedience or suffering.
    • In what ways has God used suffering in your life for your good?
5. Pray that God will continue to teach you regarding His sovereignty. Then ask God to help you be gripped by His works.

During the Session Part 2 (45 minutes)

1. Point members to the DVD Message Notes on page 76 and view DVD Group Session 5 (21:19).

2. Guide the group to follow the instructions under Responding to the Message (p. 77).
3. View the DVD segment It Happened to Me Session 5 (3:56).
4. Invite a volunteer to pray for your group to be gripped by God's works this next week.

GROUP SESSION 6

Before the Session

Set up the room, check your television/DVD player to make sure they are working properly, review the following session plans and determine which additional questions or activities would be most helpful to your group if time permits you to use them.

During the Session Part I (45 minutes)

1. Open the session with prayer or invite a volunteer to pray.
2. Ask members to turn to page 96 and follow the Discussion Guide to process what they have studied this week.

    As time allows use questions or activities from the following list to continue processing the lessons studied this past week.
3. Share your responses to the following activities:
    • Recite Isaiah 55:11 from memory (activity 1, p. 79.
    • Activity 4, p. 95
4. Review the following content:
    • How would you describe God's amazing satisfaction? (p. 81ff)
    • How would you describe God's abundant pardon? (p. 85ff)
    • How would you describe accomplished truth that we find in God's Word? (p. 91ff)
5. Invite a volunteer to pray in response to what God is doing in your group and for the upcoming teaching segment about worship.

During the Session Part 2 (45 minutes)

1. Point members to the DVD Message Notes on page 96 and view DVD Group Session 6 (21:23).
2. Guide the group to follow the instructions under Responding to the Message (p. 97).
3. View the DVD segment It Happened to Me Session 4 (8:55).
4. Invite a volunteer to pray for your group to be gripped by the worship of God this next week.

GROUP SESSION 7

Before the Session

Set up the room, check your television/DVD player to make sure they are working properly, review the following session plans and determine which additional questions or activities would be most helpful to your group if time permits you to use them.

During the Session Part I (45 minutes)

1. Open the session with prayer or invite a volunteer to pray.
2. Ask members to turn to page 116 and follow the Discussion Guide to process what they have studied this week.

   As time allows use questions or activities from the following list to continue processing the lessons studied this past week.
3. Share your responses to the following activities:
   • Recite Isaiah 58:2 from memory (activity 1, p. 99).
   • Activity 3, p. 99
   • Activity 6, p. 101 and why?
   • Activity 3, p. 104—invite volunteers to share a relationship they have that needs reconciliation. Take time to pray for each one.
4. Review the following content:
   • What are five things God promises to do to ignite our worship? (p. 110ff)
5. Discuss the following questions:
   • What do you sense we can do individually and corporately as a church to enhance our worship of the Lord?
6. Invite group members to pray in response to what they sense God is saying to them about worship. Allow time for several to pray.

During the Session Part 2 (45 minutes)

1. Point members to the DVD Message Notes on page 116 and view the DVD Group Session 7 (20:39).
2. Guide the group to follow the instructions under Responding to the Message (p. 117).
3. View the DVD segment It Happened to Me Session 4 (7:17).
4. Invite a volunteer to pray for your group to be gripped by their identity in God this next week.

GROUP SESSION 8

This session does not have a DVD teaching segment. You will spend this session processing what you have studied this week and closing out your study of *Gripped by the Greatness of God*.

Before the Session

Set up the room, review the following session plans and determine which questions or activities would be most helpful to your group. If your group will continue to meet using a new resource, be prepared to share information about the next study.

During the Session

1. Open the session with prayer or invite a volunteer to pray.
2. As time allows use questions or activities from the following list to process the lessons studied this past week.
3. Share your responses to the following activities:
   • Recite Isaiah 43:1 from memory (activity 1, p. 119).
   • Activity 3, p. 119
   • Activity 8, p. 121
   • Activities 6 and 7, p. 136
4. Review the following content:
   • What are three pseudo solutions to counter negative affects of poor identity thoughts? (p. 120)
   • What are five characteristics of God that affect our identity thoughts? (p. 122)
   • What are the five corresponding identity thoughts? five attitudes?
5. Discuss the following questions:
   • What have you learned or experienced about your identity in God this week that has been most meaningful or life changing?
   • How do identity thoughts affect attitudes and actions?
   • Which of the identity thought combination was most meaningful to you and why?
6. Invite volunteers to express their praise, worship, and thanksgiving to God for what He has revealed of Himself and ways He has been at work in your lives. Encourage them to pray more than once as you pray conversationally. Close with a time of praying for each other. You may want to pray for each person individually. Ask, "How may we pray for you?" and then pray.

Two Ways to Earn Credit
for Studying LifeWay Christian Resources Material

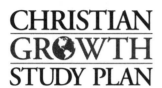

Christian Growth Study Plan resources are available for course credit for personal growth and church leadership training.

Courses are designed as plans for personal spiritual growth and for training current and future church leaders. To receive credit, complete the book, material, or activity. Respond to the learning activities or attend group sessions, when applicable, and show your work to your pastor, staff member, or church leader. Then go to *www.lifeway.com/CGSP,* or call the toll-free number for instructions for receiving credit and your certificate of completion.

CONTACT INFORMATION:
Christian Growth Study Plan
One LifeWay Plaza, MSN 117
Nashville, TN 37234
CGSP info line 1-800-968-5519
www.lifeway.com/CGSP
To order resources 1-800-458-2772

For information about studies in the Christian Growth Study Plan, refer to the current catalog online at the CGSP Web address. This program and certificate are free LifeWay services to you.

Need a CEU?

Receive Continuing Education Units (CEUs) when you complete group Bible studies by your favorite LifeWay authors.

CONTACT INFORMATION:
CEU Coordinator
One LifeWay Plaza, MSN 150
Nashville, TN 37234
Info line 1-800-968-5519
www.lifeway.com/CEU

Some studies are approved by the Association of Christian Schools International (ACSI) for CEU credits. Do you need to renew your Christian school teaching certificate? Gather a group of teachers or neighbors and complete one of the approved studies. Then go to *www.lifeway.com/CEU* to submit a request form or to find a list of ACSI-approved LifeWay studies and conferences. Book studies must be completed in a group setting. Online courses approved for ACSI credit are also noted on the course list. The administrative cost of each CEU certificate is only $10 per course.

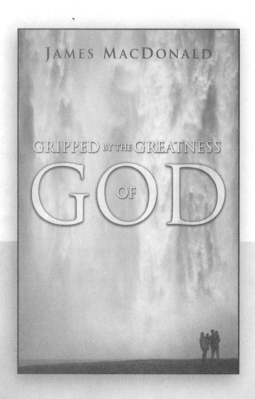